IAGO

SOME APPROACHES
TO THE ILLUSION
OF HIS MOTIVATION

127-8

Also by
STANLEY EDGAR HYMAN

FLANNERY O'CONNOR

STANDARDS
A Chronicle of Books for Our Time

THE PROMISED END
Essays and Reviews, 1942–1962

NATHANAEL WEST

THE TANGLED BANK
Darwin, Marx, Frazer and Freud as Imaginative Writers

POETRY AND CRITICISM
Four Revolutions in Literary Taste

THE ARMED VISION
A Study in the Methods of Modern Literary Criticism

IAGO

SOME APPROACHES
TO THE ILLUSION
OF HIS
MOTIVATION

BY
STANLEY EDGAR HYMAN

IAGO: *For I am nothing if not Criticall.*

ELEK LONDON

Published in Great Britain in 1971
by
ELEK BOOKS LIMITED
2 All Saints Street
London N1

ISBN 0 236 15426 5

Designed by Harry Ford
First published in the United States by
Atheneum Publishing Company of New York

Printed in Great Britain
By Unwin Brothers Limited
The Gresham Press, Old Woking, Surrey, England
A member of the Staples Printing Group

For

PHOEBE PETTINGELL

who is many things, and *critical*

ACKNOWLEDGMENTS

MUCH OF this book was written, with a comically appropriate fitness, in a thatched cottage in Great Shelford, England. It was begun and finished on Denby Island, Three Lakes, Wisconsin, under ideal writing conditions, thanks to the kindness of my hostess, Mrs. Donaldson Pettingell. I wrote *Iago* on a John Simon Guggenheim Memorial Foundation fellowship, for which I am most grateful to President Gordon N. Ray and the officers of the Foundation. For much of the time I was also on a sabbatical leave from Bennington College, for which I cordially thank President Edward J. Bloustein, the members of the Board of Trustees, and my colleagues in the Literature Division, who kindly assumed my share of the load. I am profoundly grateful to my friends and present and former colleagues: Kenneth Burke, Howard Nemerov, Herbert Weisinger, and C. L. Barber for recommending me for the Guggenheim fellowship; Professor Barber, Barbara Herrnstein Smith, and Norman Holland for reading the manuscript in whole or in part and saving me from many of the consequences of ignorance; Walter Lehrman for his careful and scholarly proofreading and correcting errors and omissions, as well as for kindly compiling the index. Other friends and colleagues, far too many to list, provided me with scholarly materials and information; the kind of discussion and dialectic interplay from which (as this book seeks to demonstrate) truth sometimes emerges was provided by my classes in Shakespeare at Bennington College and, during a visiting year, at the State University of New York at Buffalo, and my audiences and hosts at various colleges and universities where parts of this material were delivered as lectures. My thanks go to the editors of *The Centennial Review* and *Shenandoah* for allowing me to reprint parts of this book which originally appeared in their pages. Harry Ford, my friend and editor at Atheneum, has been boundlessly encouraging, and the staff there has kindly helped in a variety of fashions. The contributions of my beloved wife, which range from the earliest discussions of the idea, to writing an appendix of learned and admirable operatic criticism, are most inadequately acknowledged by the dedication.

Bennington College, Bennington, Vermont   S. E. H.
July 1970

CONTENTS

IAGO

SOME APPROACHES
TO THE ILLUSION
OF HIS MOTIVATION

INTRODUCTION

I T IS OFTEN useful to begin by defining a work
negatively. This book is not an interpretation of
Shakespeare's play *Othello*, nor an analysis of the
character of Iago in it, nor even an explanation of
what Coleridge called his "motiveless malignity." I
am no Shakespeare scholar, nor indeed any scholar
at all, and such works would be beyond my powers
even were they within my intention. What I *have*
attempted to write is a display of pluralist literary
criticism, a cause I have been advocating for over
two decades now, since my first book, *The Armed
Vision*, in 1948. I have chosen the problem of what
motivates Iago, a question over which a great deal
of critical ink has been spilled, as a good display case
for pluralist criticism: we can watch different critical
vocabularies asking the question within their own
system of terms, and getting an answer, not surprisingly, also within their own system of terms. In
my view, putting these limited and partial—or overstated and reductive—answers together, on the theory
of the symposium, that truth has a good chance to
emerge out of the mutually corrective interplay of

3

part-truth and error, one gets a richer sense of the critical problem—ultimately, of the literary work—than any single critical vocabulary or method can give.

The five critical vocabularies which I have chosen to display here are not the principal critical methods, nor my own favorites, merely the ones most obviously invited by the text—other texts would best utilize other methods. I have concluded each chapter with a look at some of the scholars and critics who have taken that approach to the problem, or come some part of the way. This is not a comprehensive survey of the literature, merely a random sampling for comparison and some sense of intellectual history. Thus all five readings are my own work, although I have tried to make them as faithful as possible to the principles of this or that critical method. Beyond the confines of this pluralist effort, I do not endorse any one of them as *the* approach or reading. Most of my critical samples before 1886 are from Horace Howard Furness' *A New Variorum Edition of Shakespeare: Othello*; later quotations are cited individually.

Having gotten possible misconceptions about the nature of the book out of the way (insofar as one can ever do such a thing with even partial success), the next thicket calling for the machete is the question of Iago's motivation. Let me say this as firmly as possible: as a character in a play, not a person, Iago has no motivation. His entire existence consists of words on a page: he has no psychology, no character or personality, no history (he had no past before the play began, and has no future after it ends).* All this being so, why talk about his motivation? Because things are not quite so simple. The dramatist has a problem, of which the best discussion is still the fifteenth chapter of Aristotle's *Poetics*, that when he has created a plot (*mythos*) he must create personages with such a character (*ethos*) as will make their actions seem credible. Aristotle suggests four rules of thumb for character: that it be dramatically good (*chrestos*), that is, effective; that it be suitable (*harmoxo*); that it be similar (*homoios*) to what the dramatic situation makes likely; and, finally, that it be consistent (*homalon*). In short, the personage on the stage (or page) must act and speak *as though* he had a psychology, a personality, a history going back to birth, and so forth, in order to make his behavior, or his share of the play's action, credible and dramatically effective. That is, Shake-

---

* L. C. Knights, who did so much to kill off the notion of Bradleian "character" in "How Many Children Had Lady Macbeth?" in 1933, has somewhat restored the balance in another lecture, "The Question of Character in Shakespeare" in 1959, reprinted in *Approaches to Shakespeare* (1964), edited by Norman Rabkin. The author writes: "And of course you can't get away from the term. Not only does the ordinary theatregoer or reader need it to explain his enjoyment, but even critics least in sympathy with Bradley at times naturally and necessarily define their sense of significance in terms appropriate to living people. . . . The notion of 'character,' in some sense, has not disappeared, and is not going to disappear, from Shakespeare criticism. What we need to do is simply to clear up our minds about it, to make our handling of the term both more flexible and more precise."

speare must create the illusion (again by means of words on the page) that such a figure as Iago is motivated in everything that he does. In this book, whenever I refer to "motivation," "consciousness," or any of the words which relate to such concepts, that is what I mean and all that I mean: the dramatic illusion that Shakespeare has created to make his tragedy work effectively.

"Motivation" and "illusion" having been explained, the other term in my subtitle, "approach," should be easier. It is a metaphor which credits a critical method or vocabulary with taking the writer (or reader) nearer to the literary work being analyzed. Bringing us closer is assumed to be a good, in order that we may see the literary work more clearly; the figure is thus another form of Coleridge's metaphor for critical method, "the armed vision" or microscope, which Richards has rephrased, with a fine pun, as a "speculative instrument." Approaches are really sets of terms, and may thus be good or bad (that is, effective or ineffective in getting us nearer to the work and able to see it more clearly) and they may be used well or ill by individual critics, depending on such intangibles as the critic's taste, tact, mother-wit, and other qualities which have not been pervasive in our literary criticism in recent decades. The different critical methods or vocabularies which I display in this book sometimes quote the same passage from the play, but inevitably read and use it differently, in terms of their different assumptions and purposes.

6

Introduction

Each of these chapters, except the central third one, more or less starts at the beginning of the play and runs through to the end, accumulating its significances as it goes. The third chapter has been broadened to include the figure of Prospero from *The Tempest* as well (here my sources of early scholarship and criticism are the *Tempest Variorum*), since the contrast with Iago seems to me extremely revealing. This chapter has also been organized on a different principle, by topic rather than sequentially, mainly to break the monotony of five runs-through of one play focussed on one character. I have used the text of the First Folio, making what has seemed to me a necessary minimum of modernizations: I have freely exchanged U and V, as well as I, J and Y; I have abandoned the long S and the odd habit of italicizing personal names; I have put spaces around parentheses where the typesetter did not, corrected obvious typographical errors, and spelled out the abbreviations, including the confusing convention of spelling "aye" as "I." Otherwise I print the text as it appears in 1623, with all its inconsistencies of spelling and punctuation, in the hope that we thus come as close as we can (that is, "approach" again) to Shakespeare's own manuscript text. The whole book, in fact, has a secondary purpose which may be seen as similar: to open up and display as much as possible of the richness and complexity of an intriguing question concerning a fascinating character in a great work of literature.

7

[1]

THE APPROACH here is genre criticism, the history of literary forms, which deals with Iago as traditional stage villain. In these terms, what motivates him is the need to war perpetually against love and happiness, trust and virtue, harmony and beauty, and all other manifestations of order and value;* this perpetual war is the theatrical convention of his role. The role goes back at least as far as the earliest medieval mystery and miracle plays, and continues far beyond Elizabethan times.

The traditional villain of the English stage has a number of fixed and easily recognizable characteristics. The basic one is the deceit and hypocrisy with which he misleads his dupes. We can see this as early as Mak the sheep stealer in the Towneley Second Shepherds' Play, assuring the shepherds

As I am true and lele, to God here I pray,
That this be the fyrst mele that I shalle ete this day.

---

* Bradley in *Shakespearean Tragedy* (1950) says that Iago "has a spite against goodness in men," and Robert B. Heilman in *Magic in the Web* (1956) has added, by way of supplement: "He is a concentration of all the pure spite at the heart."

The villain Dissimulation in Bale's *King John*, who intends to poison the king, addresses him thus:

Now Jesus preserve your worthye and excellent grace,
For doubtless there is a very angelyck face.
Now forsoth and God, I woulde thynke my self in
      heaven,
If I myght remayne with yow but yeares alevyn.
I woulde covete here none other felicyte.

In Thomas Kyd's *The Spanish Tragedie*, the chief villain, Lorenzo, who has prevented Hieronimo from getting to the king to tell him of Lorenzo's wicked murder of Hieronimo's son, assures his father:

Your-selfe, my lord, hath seene his passions,
That ill beseemde the presence of a king;
And, for I pittied him in his distresse,
I helde him thence with kinde and curteous words,
As free from malice to Hieronimo
As to my soule, my lord.

As late as Marlowe's *The Jew of Malta*, Barabas tells Mathias, who will soon be one of his victims,

Oh, heaven forbid I should have such a thought.
Pardon me though I weepe.

Accompanying this falsity to the victims and dupes there is the villain's proud candor regarding his real nature and intentions in asides or soliloquies to the audience. Again Mak furnishes a ready example, in a boast to his wife:

9

I am worthy my mete,
For in a strate can I gett
More then thay that swynke and swette
    All the long day.
Thus it felle to my lotte, Gylle, I had sich grace.

Politick Persuasion, the Vice in *Patient and Meek Grissell*, announces:

I will not cease prively her confusion to worke,
For under Honnie the proverbe saith poyson maye
    lurke:
So though I simulate externally love to pretend,
My love shall turne to mischife, I warrant you in the
    end.

Villuppo, the secondary villain in *The Spanish Tragedie*, after he has told his brazen lie that gets Alexandro sentenced to death, remarks amiably to the audience:

        Thus have I with an envious forged tale
        Deceived the king, betraid mine enemy,
        And hope for guerdon of my villany.

Lorenzo, the principal villain, explains in an aside,

    Why, so! this fits our former pollicie;
    And thus experience bids the wise to deale.
    I lay the plot, he prosecutes the point;
    I set the trap, he breakes the worthles twigs,
    And sees not that wherewith the bird was limde.

Finally, Barabas the Jew has any number of long monologues in which he proudly proclaims his crimes, of which the single line, "Sometimes I goe about and poyson wells," should be adequate illustration.

These two characteristics of the traditional stage villain are central to Iago. However, he is only candid with the audience about his nature and purposes, not his motives—since he has no motives which are not ontological. Other features of the traditional role which he does not share (because they were largely extinct by 1604) need detain us only briefly. The stage villain is a ranter and a roarer, like Erode in the Coventry Corpus Christi play dealing with the Slaughter of the Innocents, who rages typically:

A-nothur wey? owt! owt! owtt!
    Hath those fawls trayturs done me this ded?
I stampe! I stare! I loke all abowtt!
    Myght I them take, I schuld them bren at a glede!

In other cases he degenerates into a burlesque figure, such as the Beelzebub who enters the Lutterworth St. George play announcing cheerily:

> In comes I, old Beelzebub;
> Over my shoulder I carry my club,
> And in my hand a frying-pan
> Pleased to get all the money I can.

(One development of this characteristic is the villain's comic sneering aside, which we see on occasion with Iago, at least in regard to Rodorigo.)

11

Like these traditional figures, Iago exposes his villainy to the audience in boastful soliloquies. A classic example comes near the end of the first scene, just before Iago leaves the stage. He says, of Othello:

> Though I do hate him as I do hell paines,
> Yet, for necessitie of present life,
> I must show out a Flag, and signe of Love,
> (Which is indeed but signe)

This not only exposes Iago to the audience, but does so with gusto and wit, since he is Othello's flag-bearer or *ensign* ("ancient" in the play), and is raising his flag or sign of hatred to the audience as he dissembles love for Othello.

Two principal characteristics of the stage villain, as these soliloquies make clear, are exaggerated wickedness and hypocrisy. The extreme wickedness is early revealed in the first scene in a simile Iago uses when instructing Rodorigo how to cry out to rouse Brabantio. He says:

> Doe, with like timerous accent, and dire yell,
> As when (by Night and Negligence) the Fire
> Is spied in populous Cities,

Gould's account in *The Tragedian* of how the actor Junius Brutus Booth performed this speech gives a good sense of the aura of stage villainy in the imagery. He writes:

> J. B. Booth uttered these words, without heat, with a devilish unconcern, as if pleased with

the fancy of terror and dismay; and playing, meanwhile, with his sword-hilt or pulling at his gauntlets. He then strikes on the door of Brabantio's house, and speaking through the keyhole, sounds the resonant alarm, 'What ho, Brabantio.' Yet in saying this, we felt his mind was 'playing with some inward bait.' The duplicity, the double nature, the devil in him, was subtly manifest.

The stage villain's edifice of duplicity and hypocrisy is revealed to Rodorigo (and the audience) all through the first scene. The earliest revelation is a <u>bold</u> pun on "service," when Iago says "I follow him, to serve my turne upon him." It is all summed up in an early speech of self-revelation. Iago explains:

> Were I the Moore, I would not be Iago:
> In following him, I follow but my selfe.
> Heaven is my Judge, not I for love and dutie,
> But seeming so, for my peculiar end:
> For when my outward Action doth demonstrate
> The native act, and figure of my heart
> In Complement externe, 'tis not long after
> But I will weare my heart upon my sleeve
> For Dawes to pecke at; I am not what I am.

When Othello enters in the second scene, we observe Iago's duplicity in action. Although later in the play we see him as a cold-blooded assassin, a smiler with a knife, he begins the scene by proclaiming to Othello his scruples against killing. Iago says of Brabantio:

Though in the trade of Warre I have slaine men,
Yet do I hold it very stuffe o'th'conscience
To do no contriv'd Murder: I lacke Iniquitie
Sometime to do me service. Nine, or ten times
I had thought t'have yerk'd him here under the
      Ribbes.

Iago goes on to explain that when Brabantio insulted
Othello, Iago restrained himself "with the little godlinesse I have." This latter is a lovely phrase, since it
disclaims all but a minimum of godliness, in Shakespeare's familiar character of the honest, bluff soldier;
beneath that it proclaims that he is in fact too godly to
kill; and it simultaneously assures the audience that
he is in fact quite ungodly enough to kill on the in-
stant. Later in the scene Iago swears "By Janus,"
quite the proper god for the double-faced stage villain,
and perhaps Janus is all the godliness he has.

    In the third scene, the confrontation with the Duke
and the Venetian senators, Iago, quite properly, is
mostly silent. When Othello finally introduces him to
the Duke it is with <u>heavy unconscious irony</u>: "A man
he is of honesty and trust." Just before he exits,
Othello addresses Iago, in the first of many such salu-
tations, as "Honest Iago." He then leaves Iago alone on
the stage with Rodorigo, and, after Rodorigo has been
instructed and has departed, Iago remains for another
villainous soliloquy to the audience, in which we hear
him develop his plot further. Iago muses:

Cassio's a proper man: Let me see now,
To get his Place, and to plume up my will

In double Knavery. How? How? Let's see.
After some time, to abuse Othello's eares,
That he is too familiar with his wife:
He hath a person, and a smooth dispose
To be suspected: fram'd to make women false.
The Moore is of a free, and open Nature,
That thinkes men honest, that but seeme to be so,
And will as tenderly be lead by th'Nose
As Asses are:
I have't: it is engendred: Hell, and Night,
Must bring this monstrous Birth, to the world's light.

When Iago enters with Desdemona in the first scene of the second act, Cassio addresses him as "Good Ancient" and "good Iago," with the adjective carrying the same heavy irony as "honest." When Othello arrives shortly afterwards, he proclaims his great love to Desdemona, and, as they kiss, he expresses the hope that the kisses will "the greatest discords be / That ere our hearts shall make." Iago immediately proclaims in a prose stage whisper, in what G. Wilson Knight has shown to be the central image of the play, his plan for the untuning of the Othello music:

Oh you are well tun'd now. But Ile set downe the peggs that make this Musicke, as honest as I am.

This is a particularly interesting use of "honest," among the fifty-two examples of "honest" and "honesty" in the play, classified by William Empson in his brilliant chapter "Honest in *Othello*" in *The Structure of Complex Words*. Among other things it means:

that he will untune the Othello music however honest (that is, faithful) Othello thinks him; that he will do so by means of his hypocritical "honesty"; and that he can honestly assure the audience that it will honestly be done. Later in the scene, Iago gives another description of Othello's goodness, along the lines of his soliloquy at the end of Act I, which further defines his own villainy by contrast. He says:

> The Moore (howbeit that I endure him not)
> Is of a constant, loving, Noble Nature.

If Othello is Iago's vulnerable antithesis, Rodorigo is his despised tool, whom he describes as "this poore Trash of Venice." He concludes the scene with a characteristic ringing couplet of the stage villain, proclaiming, about his unformed plot:

> Tis heere: but yet confus'd,
> Knaveries plaine face, is never seene, till us'd.

In the second scene of the act, Othello again describes Iago as "most honest," and Cassio again addresses him as "good Iago." Iago, as soon as he is alone on the stage once more, sneers villainously at "my sicke Foole Rodorigo," and as Cassio and Montano, the governor of Cyprus, approach (with Cassio drunk by Iago's doing), Iago soliloquizes grandiloquently:

> If Consequence do but approve my dreame,
> My Boate sailes freely, both with winde and Streame.

As the two fight, and Montano is wounded, Iago pretends to try to calm them, and when Othello and his attendants enter, Iago lectures them both, with repulsive hypocrisy:

Have you forgot all place of sense and dutie?
Hold. The Generall speaks to you: hold for shame.

(One has only to recall Iago's cynical definitions of both "sense" and "duty.") Othello then addresses Iago:

Honest Iago, that lookes dead with greeving,
Speake: who began this? On thy love I charge thee.

In the ensuing discussion (foreshadowing the Desdemona main plot) Iago manages to indict Cassio in the guise of defending him, and Othello concludes:

I know Iago.
Thy honestie, and love doth mince this matter,
Making it light to Cassio:

In his next words, Othello dismisses Cassio summarily. When he is next alone on the stage with Cassio, Iago says to him ambiguously, "And good Lieutenant, I thinke, you thinke I love you," and advises him to plead his suit to Desdemona, dismissing Cassio's praise for his advice with "I protest in the sinceritie of Love, and honest kindnesse." When Cassio exits, again saluting his treacherous undoer as "honest Iago," Iago is left alone on the stage for another of his villainous self-revelations to the audience. He first asks rhetorically:

And what's he then,
That sayes I play the Villaine?
When this advise is free I give, and honest,
Proball to thinking, and indeed the course
To win the Moore againe.

As he continues, he asks again "How am I then a Villaine?" and goes on to expose his real intentions:

For whiles this honest Foole
Plies Desdemona, to repaire his Fortune,
And she for him, pleades strongly to the Moore,
Ile powre this pestilence into his eare:
That she repeales him, for her bodies Lust

("Repeals" is an old form of "recalls.") After Rodorigo has entered to complain and been sent off with more glowing promises, Iago is left onstage to conclude the act with still another traditional soliloquy of the stage villain. He says:

Two things are to be done:
My Wife must move for Cassio to her Mistris:
Ile set her on my selfe, a while, to draw the Moor
    apart,
And bring him jumpe, when he may Cassio finde
Soliciting his wife: Aye, that's the way:
Dull not Device, by coldnesse, and delay.

In the third scene of Act III, when Æmilia assures Desdemona that her husband is grieved by Cassio's fate, Desdemona adopts the general view of Iago and

18

comments, "Oh that's an honest Fellow." Later in the scene, Iago begins the serious business of his principal villainy, the destruction of Desdemona by arousing Othello's jealousy. He begins it with the characteristic hypocrisy of his traditional role, warning:

Oh, beware my Lord, of jealousie,
It is the greene-ey'd Monster, which doth mocke
The meate it feeds on.

(The critical debate on these famous lines is probably the fullest, and certainly the funniest, for *Othello*—Zachary Jackson's explanation that what is meant is a green-eyed mouse or mouster is one of the high points of nitwit scholarship—but there has been no agreement about the key words: whether "mock" means "sneers at," "toys with," or what; whether "the meat it feeds on" is the victim, suspicion, or what. As is usual with Shakespeare, however absurd it is to say, the purport of the passage is perfectly clear even where many of the words mystify.) Iago goes on in the scene to warn Othello, "Looke to your wife, observe her well with Cassio," and, turning on her his own ambiguous label (here meaning "chaste"), assures Othello (with a wonderful double negative) "I do not think but Desdemona's honest." As Iago separates from Othello to leave, Othello picks up the word, musing:

This honest Creature (doubtlesse)
Sees, and knowes more, much more than he unfolds.

19

When Iago has left the stage, Othello continues, "This Fellow's of exceeding honesty." Later in the scene, after Æmilia has given Desdemona's lost handkerchief to Iago, and has been dismissed, he proclaims to the audience:

> I will in Cassio's Lodging loose this Napkin,
> And let him finde it.

He then adds gleefully, "The Moore already changes with my poyson." When Othello reenters, momentarily less gullible, and demands some evidence of Desdemona's betrayal, Iago goes all melodramatic about the hard fate of the truthful in this world, crying out, "Take note, take note (O World) / To be direct and honest, is not safe," and announces that he will never again try to help a friend with the loving truth. Othello immediately backs down: "Nay stay: thou should'st be honest." Iago again denies that he wishes to say any more, but explains that he is "Prick'd too't by foolish Honesty, and Love." The scene ends with Othello entirely convinced.

Iago appears only briefly in the fourth scene, to bring Cassio to Desdemona, egg him on to plead his case to her, and then leave, on the pretext that Othello is so rarely angry that if he is so now, Iago must go to mollify him.

In the first scene of the fourth act, Iago finally succeeds in untuning the Othello music, and Othello, babbling madly, falls into a trance. Iago stands over him to make the most bombastic, didactic, and melodramatic of all his stage villain speeches. He cries out:

Worke on,
My Medicine workes. Thus credulous Fooles are
    caught,
And many worthy, and chast Dames even thus,
(All guiltlesse) meete reproach.

Othello revives, and Iago sends him off to prepare for the next revelation, which will set down the pegs a turn or two more. Iago then soliloquizes, "Now will I question Cassio of Bianca." Othello watches from concealment, thinking the questioning will be about Desdemona, and Iago announces triumphantly, of Cassio: "As he shall smile, Othello shall go mad." Convinced, Othello resolves to poison Desdemona, and Iago proposes, in a height of melodramatic villainy,

Do it not with poyson, strangle her in her bed,
Even the bed she hath contaminated.

At the end of the scene, when Lodovico, the emissary from Venice, inquires about Othello's mad ranting and raving, Iago answers with his usual loyal reticence that charges more than any charges could:

Alas, alas:
It is not honestie in me to speake
What I have seene, and knowne.

In the second scene, with the most revolting hypocrisy, he reassures Desdemona: "Go in, and weepe not:

all things shall be well." (Shakespeare may have been familiar with *Revelations of Divine Love* by Dame Julian of Norwich, whose "Sin is behovely, but all shall be well, and all manner of thing shall be well," has been popularized in our time by T. S. Eliot.) Iago's next move as stage villain is to encourage Rodorigo to kill Cassio. He proposes "the removing of Cassio"; explains, in answer to Rodorigo's query, "Why, by making him uncapable of Othello's place: knocking out his braines"; then instructs and assures Rodorigo: "if you will watch his going thence (which I will fashion to fall out betweene twelve and one) you may take him at your pleasure. I will be neere to second your Attempt, and he shall fall betweene us."

In the first scene of the fifth act, the attempted assassination is set up. Rodorigo is left in his hiding-place with unsheathed rapier, but, not quite a model of bravery, he implores Iago, "Be neere at hand, I may miscarry in't." Iago assures him, with his familiar hypocrisy, "Heere, at thy hand," and then in a soliloquy to the audience, reveals his nasty contempt for Rodorigo and the utter ruthlessness of his real hopes. He says:

I have rub'd this yong Quat almost to the sense,
And he grows angry. Now, whether he kill Cassio,
Or Cassio him, or each do kill the other,
Every way makes my gaine.

("Quat" is a pimple.) Iago wishes Rodorigo dead because he will want back all the money he has given Iago to win Desdemona for him. As for Cassio:

If Cassio do remaine,
He hath a dayly beauty in his life,
That makes me ugly: and besides, the Moore
May unfold me to him: there stand I in much perill:
No, he must dye.

When Cassio enters, and he and Rodorigo have
wounded each other (or Iago has wounded Cassio),
Othello appears, as instructed by Iago, whom he now
calls "O brave Iago, honest, and just," under the im-
pression that Iago has slain Cassio on Othello's behalf.
When Iago, who has temporarily left the stage, returns, he is about to dispatch Cassio (in a reading of
Booth's which I share) when he sees Lodovico and
Gratiano approach, and instead talks sympathetically
to the wounded Cassio, learns that his attacker lies
nearby wounded, and, piously crying, "Oh murd'rous
Slave! O Villaine!" he stabs Rodorigo to death. Iago
concludes the scene with the standard crisis image of
his tradition (Lorenzo says, "now stands our fortune
on a tickle point"):

This is the night
That either makes me, or foredoes me quight.

In the second scene of the act, and the play's last
scene, the final confrontation of Othello and Desdemona, in which he smothers her, Othello tells Desdemona that Cassio can no longer admit or deny anything, since his mouth has been stopped by "Honest
Iago." After the murder, Othello informs Æmilia that
he learned of Desdemona's adultery with Cassio from

her husband, "An honest man he is," and adds, more desperately, "My Friend, thy Husband; honest, honest Iago." We see no more of Iago as traditional stage villain in the play. When he returns for the last time, to be exposed, judged, and sentenced, he no longer wears that mask.

There can be no doubt that Shakespeare was familiar with the stock villain of the religious plays, which were the principal drama of England for two centuries. The great local cycles of mystery plays were still being performed at least past the death of Elizabeth. There is a clear reminiscence of *The Harrowing of Hell* in the Porter scene in *Macbeth*, and Falstaff's attributes are openly borrowed from the Vices of a number of different morality plays. Shakespeare was almost unique, however, in using the tradition of the stage villain with scarcely any humor or comic ranting (at least here: the Bastard in *Lear* has plenty of humor, and Richard III rants like any medieval Herod), as he wrote in *King Lear* the only version of the "Cinderella" story (in the "Love Like Salt" variant) with an unhappy ending. (The reason for the relative humorlessness of Iago as stage villain will be clearer in the next chapter; the inexplicable mystery of his genius is the only adequate reason for the unhappy ending of *King Lear*.)

Little has been written about Iago as traditional stage villain, although every critic has been aware of this aspect of the character (emphasis on it was the dominant acting tradition for the role until our century), because it is usual to think of the convention as a style in which Iago's otherwise-motivated villainy is expressed, rather than as the motivation itself. However, as Bradley says, "Iago's plot is Iago's character in action." As he is, in one of his aspects, a stage villain, so must he do and say stagily villainous things. Beyond that lurks Shakespeare's own motivation: he must unfold his dramatic action, the untuning of the Othello music.

The only comprehensive treatment of the subject with which I am familiar appears in *Shakespeare and the Allegory of Evil* (1958), by Bernard Spivack, subtitled "The History of a Metaphor in Relation to His Major Villains." Spivack's thesis is that Iago preserves many traces of the Vice of the old morality plays, and that this ancestry motivates him and solves the problem of his lack of credible naturalistic motivation. Developing arguments used in Heilman's *Magic in the Web*, Spivack does a brilliant job in showing that Iago's expressed motivations are unconvincing, contradicted by other remarks, and in fact consistently forgotten as soon as they are mentioned. As the Vice, Spivack writes, "His aim is the moral and spiritual ruin of his victim in order that he may demonstrate thereby the destructive force and characteristic effect of the evil he personifies." Iago's typical act is "the sly insinuation of moral evil into the human breast." He too carries on "the Vice's hereditary work," which is, as Politick Persuasion explains it in *Patient and Meek Grissell*, "To vexe and harme those wightes, whose lives most vertuous are." Spivack's book is a most comprehensive and useful one, and I am indebted to it for some of my historical examples above, and for a considerable part of my understanding of Iago's traditional stage background.

What keeps *Shakespeare and the Allegory of Evil* from being the definitive example of this approach, and thus making this chapter unnecessary, are limitations which seem almost inevitable in any pioneering theorist's natural overstatement of his case. One is that Spivack finds Iago far too funny (since his predecessors are often extremely funny) to satisfy a modern reader of *Othello*. Except in one place, Spivack writes, "his emotions are simply variations on the monolithic passion of laughter." Elsewhere he speaks of Iago's general "jocularity," "the mirth that is Iago's only real emotion"; at the end of Act II the figure "now grins at us in the full light"; elsewhere his features appear "wrinkled in mocking laughter." At the end, having shown the evolution of the convention, Spivack tries to mitigate this tone ("It is no longer the coarse hilarity of the Vice of old, but if not loud it remains deep"), but the effort comes too late.

A second weakness, perhaps more important, is that Spivack's genetic approach, *within itself*, splits Iago into two and breaks the back of the play. He tells us that Iago's "character . . . can be unwoven into two very dissimilar roles governed by two different motive principles." In Iago's second role, as the Vice, "he is not indigenous to the play and not a member of the human world it displays." Spivack writes in his concluding chapter: "Iago's hatred, in short, having become isolated from its allegorical predication, survives unattached."

Another limitation is that Spivack insists that his is the principal explanation, and subordinates to it all other approaches. To name only those with which I am concerned in this volume: He says that Iago as Satan or a figuration of Satan "is an incidental metaphor leading nowhere." He admits Iago as an analogue of the artist, but it is only the artist in crime, not a caricature of the writer. Spivack writes typically (but redundantly of Iago in this case): "As for the artist himself, his characteristic achievement is to ensnare and mislead his victim, to demonstrate his power over him, and to create dissension and debate where formerly there were unity and affection." He dismisses psychological approaches as resorting "merely to psychology" or "psychological subtleties that fly out of sight of an issue which, at its base at least, is technical." He admits that Iago is a figure of the Machiavel but adds that this is mainly a "Machiavellian gloss," and summarizes: "Applied to Iago, the Machiavellian label, while supplying some prefatory enlightenment, is too general to carry us very far into the moral meaning of the role."

Finally, and this is perhaps Spivack's major limitation, the figure of the Vice from the morality plays is too reductive, leaving out too much before, after, and around it, to be a fully adequate prototype for Iago. Spivack appears to recognize this, sometimes calling him "villain" or "Vice-villain," noting the First Folio's identification of him in the cast of characters as "Iago, a Villaine," and even listing a whole series of characterizations in the play of Iago as "villain" with one or another intensifying adjective, and his acts as "villainy." Too much of Iago does not coincide with the medieval vices of the morality plays, described by Spivack thus: "these destructive forces were always dramatized as grotesque or ludicrous figures, rich and vivid in their coarseness and obscenity, their blasphemous mockery, their horseplay and raucous quarrels among themselves." Elsewhere Spivack, describing the Vice (into which the vices gradually merged), says: "His quality as a personification of evil gets its typical anthropomorphic expression through his vulgarity, insolence, cynicism, scorn, and triumphant hilarity." In his account of the evolutionary process into Elizabethan times, Spivack tries to repair this ("The horseplay and strident jeering are largely gone," the figure "becomes less of a monologuist") but the distortion of emphasis remains, and Spivack's valuable reading of Iago is no more the fully satisfactory account of the villain and his motivation than anyone else's.

[2]

M Y SECOND APPROACH is theological criticism—
that is, words about God, or, if you prefer,
Christian myth criticism; its Iago is motivated by
the fact that he is Satan or a figuration of Satan, eternally fixed in a posture of hatred of God and envy of
man. He wins the souls of men by promising to grat-
ify their desires: Rodorigo's for Desdemona, Cassio's
for his return to favor, Othello's for certainty (perhaps the certainty of guilt). The Satanic note begins
strongly in the play's first scene. Iago describes Cassio
to Rodorigo as "A Fellow almost damn'd in a faire
Wife," and whatever that mysterious description may
mean in the play (since Cassio is not married) its
meaning is clear in this context: that Cassio has a
weakness, in Iago's opinion, which invites perdition.
In theological terms, Iago's title of "ancient" is a pun:
as Satan he is ancient in evil, "Old Nick." "I am not
what I am," quoted in its context earlier, is not only
the stage villain's revelation of his duplicity; its deeper
meaning is that this villain is Satan in disguise.
Maginn, who did not explicitly equate Iago with
Satan, nevertheless shrewdly noted the direct contrast
to God. He wrote:

Can these last words be intended as a somewhat profane allusion to the title by which the Almighty reveals himself to Moses? Exod. iii, 14. I AM THAT I AM is the name of the God of truth. *I am not what I am* is, therefore, a fitting description of a premeditated liar.

Iago's instruction to Rodorigo regarding Othello, "Plague him with Flies," is proper instruction from the Lord of the Flies. Iago repeatedly suggests his identity in his shouting up to Brabantio in the scene: "Awake the snorting Cittizens with the Bell, / Or else the devill will make a Grand-sire of you"; "Sir: you are one of those that will not serve God, if the devill bid you." When Brabantio calls down, "What prophane wretch art thou?" the joke is that Iago is *that* profane wretch, the antithesis of the sacred. Iago further confesses his identity in a speech quoted in the last chapter, when he says of Othello, "Though I do hate him as I do hell paines." In its overt meaning this is the villain's dread of future torment; in its covert meaning it is Satan's hatred of present torment. Iago's last words in the scene, that Othello is at the Sagittary, "And there will I be with him," carry just the necessary suggestion of their antithesis, Christ's last words in the Gospel According to St. Matthew, "I am with you alway."

Iago's villainous speech opening the second scene, explaining that he did not kill Brabantio because "I lacke Iniquitie / Sometimes to do me service," takes

on much heavier irony as a Satanic profession of innocence, as does his subsequent remark, "with the little
godlinesse I have." Othello's later reference to "my
perfect Soule," which has so much annoyed some
commentators, has a similar heavy irony in terms of
his easy vulnerability to Satanic temptation.

Iago enters the third scene of the first act late, and
does not reveal his Satanic nature until even later,
when he is alone with Rodorigo. He then proclaims, "I
never found man that knew how to love himselfe," a
formula of separation from Christian *agape* which fa-
cilitates Satanic temptation. His subsequent instruc-
tions to Rodorigo, endlessly varying the formula "Put
Money in thy purse," are primarily in his role as the
Machiavel, to be dealt with in a later chapter, but in
theological terms they carry just the necessary suggestion of Judas' thirty pieces of silver and his role as
the bagman. The same speech contains several of
Iago's ceaseless references to what might be called his
shop talk: "If thou wilt needs damne thy selfe" and
"all the Tribe of hell." In his soliloquy at the end
of the scene, after Rodorigo has left, Iago says, of
Othello: "He holds me well, / The better shall my
purpose worke on him"—a fine demonic pronounce-
ment. His final villainous couplet has the same stink
of brimstone: "Hell, and Night, / Must bring this
monstrous Birth, to the worlds light."

In this theological or Christian analogical frame of
reference, Iago's motivation is not indiscriminate
Satanic hatred, but a focussed enmity. In the first

scene of the second act, even before Desdemona appears, an elaborate parallel begins to develop, in which she is a figuration of Jesus Christ (as other women, notably Dante's Beatrice, have been), an image of perfect innocence suffering perfect injustice. Cassio describes her to Montano as one

> That paragons description, and wilde Fame:
> One that excels the quirkes of Blazoning pens,
> And in th'essentiall Vesture of Creation,
> Do's tyre the Ingeniver.

The first two lines are ordinary Shakespeare hyperbole, such as might be applied to any human figure. There is no scholarly agreement about what the last two puzzling lines mean, but in the most plausible guesses "tyre" means either "exhaust" or "crown" the Creator, so that in either case they say that Desdemona is the crown of Creation. Christ is not a created being, in orthodox Christian doctrine, but a human figuration of Christ would be exactly that, the crown of created beings. Br. Nicholson, in a most interesting gloss on these lines printed in *Notes and Queries* in 1865 and reprinted by Furness, writes in part:

> Desdemona is represented as a being of purity and love, a female Abdiel 'mong Italian women; and hence Cassio is made to break out into such expression-seeking praise as to call her the top of creation, as creation is 'essentially' and without 'the accident' of sin, or as it was when it was

beautiful before God and pronounced to be very good.

Shortly afterward, Cassio refers to her as "The Divine Desdemona" and, as she enters, proclaims in clearly superhuman terms:

You men of Cyprus, let her have your knees.
Haile to thee Ladie: and the grace of Heaven,
Before, behinde thee, and on every hand
Enwheele thee round.

Iago's response is his usual mutter that women are "Divels being offended." As he sees Cassio take Desdemona's hand, he brightens, and amplifies his earlier image as Lord of the Flies into that of a spider:

He takes her by the palme: Aye, well said, whisper. With as little a web as this, will I ensnare as great a Fly as Cassio.

In a subsequent speech, quoted in the last chapter as an example of the stage villain, about setting down the pegs that keep the Othello music in tune, Iago is even more convincing as a Satanic figure, a force of discord which is the immortal enemy of divine or human harmony. Hudson commented on this speech:

It is worth noting that Milton's Satan relents at the prospect of ruining the happiness before him, and prefaces the deed with a gush of pity for the victims; whereas the same thought puts Iago in a transport of jubilant ferocity. Is our

33

idea of Satan's wickedness enhanced by his thus indulging such feelings, and then acting in defiance of them, or as if he had them not? or is Iago more devilish than he?

When Othello and Desdemona leave the stage, Iago turns to assuring Rodorigo that Desdemona must now love Cassio, since she could no longer love Othello. "And what delight," he asks rhetorically, "shall she have to looke on the divell?" Rodorigo denies that Desdemona could be involved with Cassio, explaining, "she's full of most bless'd condition." Iago's answer is a characteristic Satanic denial: "Bless'd figges-end. The Wine she drinkes is made of grapes. . . . Bless'd pudding." In his final soliloquy in the scene, Iago announces his intention of "practising upon his [Othello's] peace, and quiet, / Even to madnesse," an image of Hellish torment obviously related to the untuning theme.

In the second scene, Iago begins to tempt Cassio with drink, since Cassio has confessed to having "very poore, and unhappie Braines for drinking." "But one Cup," he says, "Ile drinke for you." Since Cassio has already had enough to drink, even one cup more, Iago observes in an aside, will make him quarrelsome and offensive. Later in the scene, after Cassio has fallen as a result of Iago's temptation, he is sobered, repentant, and correctly identifies drink, in Iago's context, as a kind of Satanic Eucharist. He says bitterly, "Oh thou invisible spirit of Wine, if thou hast no name to be knowne by, let us call thee Divell. . . . Oh, that men should put an Enemie in their mouthes, to steale away their Braines. That we should with joy, pleasance, revell and applause, transforme our selves into Beasts. . . . It hath pleas'd the divell drunkennesse, to give place to the divell wrath. . . . To be now a sensible man, by and by a Foole, and presently a Beast. Oh strange! Every inordinate cup is unbless'd, and the Ingredient is a divell." Iago answers, characteristically: "Come, come: good wine is a good familiar Creature." Before that, in their drinking scene, Cassio had raised the complementary subject of salvation. He remarks: "Well: heav'ns above all: and there be soules must be saved, and there be soules must not be saved. . . . For mine owne part. . . . I hope to be saved." Iago answers piously, with the deep and bitter irony of his being at that very moment in the deepest torments of Hell, "And so do I too Lieutenant." Cassio replies (with the same irony, but it is entirely the author's): "Aye: (but by your leave) not before me," and continues, "Forgive us our sinnes." During the brawl, Iago leaves to go out "and cry a Mutinie," and what he cries is "Diablo, hoa." When Othello enters, he gives the same theological interpretation to the brawl, proclaiming that "Heaven hath forbid" such murderous violence even to the pagan "Ottamittes," telling the participants that they should feel "Christian shame," and announcing that the next participant who goes at any one "Holds his soule light." Shortly afterwards, Iago blasphemously echoes Jesus' "Touch me not" and, in consoling Cassio, piously exclaims, "Marry Heaven forbid." In his soliloquy near the end of the scene and the act, Iago announces that Desdemona has so much power over Othello that she can get him to do anything:

And then for her
To win the Moore, were to renownce his Baptisme,
All Seales, and Simbols of redeemed sin.

Iago then makes the frankest revelation yet of his nature as a figuration of Satan. He says, in what resembles a simile but is actually a ritual formula:

Divinitie of hell,
When divels will the blackest sinnes put on,
They do suggest at first with heavenly shewes,
As I do now.

After outlining his plot against Desdemona, Iago continues:

So will I turne her vertue into pitch,
And out of her owne goodnesse make the Net,
That shall en-mash them all.

In Act III, scene 3, talking to Desdemona, and torn between the doubts Iago has raised and Desdemona's patent innocence and nobility, Othello states the play's theological point in capsule terms. He tells her, with an ominousness of which he appears unaware,

Perdition catch my Soule
But I do love thee: and when I love thee not,
Chaos is come againe.

36

Later, in his hypocritical defense of Cassio's honesty,
Iago falls into the feigned reluctance to speak further
which is one of his principal devices, and Othello says
(with a heavy irony of which he is quite unconscious,
and referring to himself in "friend"): "Thou do'st
conspire against thy Friend (Iago)." As he begins
his arousal of Othello's jealousy with his warning
against jealousy, Iago proclaims piously:

> Good Heaven, the Soules of all my Tribe defend
> From Jealousie.

Othello then exclaims (with great fitness to the Levit-
icus goat for Azazel), "Exchange me for a Goat," and
denies vehemently that he will pay attention "To such
exufflicate, and blow'd Surmises." "Exsufflicate" is a
most interesting word in this context. Richardson defines it in his *Dictionary* as "arising from the custom
in the Romish administration of baptism and renounc-
ing the devil and all his works, *exsufflando et despu-
endo*, by blowing and spitting him away." After Iago
has injected some more of his poison, and departs,
Othello muses that Iago "knowes all Quantities with a
learn'd Spirit / Of humane dealings," ("Humane"
here is "human"). It is a fine ironic description of the
figure of Satan, underlying words Othello means as
praise. He then cries out against what he considers to
be his cuckoldry as "this forked plague," which, with
all its richness of meaning (from the fork in the road
where he is at present to the human crotch), has the
same unconscious irony, as referring to Satan's forked
serpent tongue, cloven hooves, and traditional pitch-

37

fork. As Desdemona enters, Othello cries out, with more truth than he knows, "If she be false, Heaven mock'd it selfe." We see Iago again as a type of tempter when Æmilia, finding the handkerchief, says:

My wayward Husband hath a hundred times
Woo'd me to steale it.

When Iago has taken the handkerchief from Æmilia, and is again alone onstage explaining his intentions to the audience, he announces triumphantly that the poison he has implanted in Othello will soon "Burne like the Mines of Sulphure," a somewhat inappropriate image for poison, but a very appropriate one for hellfire. Othello promptly enters, crying out "Ha, ha, false to mee?" which refers of course to Desdemona but, in the audience's awareness, suggests Iago instead. Othello then confronts Iago, demands proof, "Occular proofe," of Desdemona's betrayal, and shifts into religious imagery of extreme significance in the context of this theological reading. He threatens Iago "by the worth of mine eternall Soule," and goes on:

If thou dost slander her, and torture me,
Never pray more: Abandon all remorse
On Horrors head, Horrors accumulate:
Do deeds to make Heaven weepe, all Earth amaz'd;
For nothing canst thou to damnation adde,
Greater then that.

This is perhaps the place to observe that in the theological parallel in which Iago is a figuration of Satan, and Desdemona a figuration of Christ, Othello is a figuration of Judas, who acts in sacrificing Christ as an agent of Satan, and whose fate is eternal damnation. Iago's answer to Othello's charge is the Devil's mock piety. "O Grace! O Heaven forgive me!" he pleads, with a familiar irony, and adds, "God buy you" ("buy" here is an old form of "be with"). When Iago finally succeeds in fully convincing Othello, by his incredibly bold invention of Cassio's dream, Othello promptly joins the Satanic forces. He proclaims to Iago:

All my fond love thus do I blow to Heaven. 'Tis gone.
Arise blacke vengeance, from the hollow hell,
Yeeld up (O Love) thy Crowne, and hearted Throne
To tyrannous Hate.

When Iago hypocritically tries to calm him, all Othello can say is "Oh blood, blood, blood." Othello then kneels down to swear his hellish vengeance, and after a moment Iago kneels with him. It is an overt and most dramatic pact with the Devil. Othello cries out "Damne her . . . O damne her, damne her," and calls Desdemona "the faire Divell." On this terrible note the scene ends.

By the next scene, as damning Desdemona and calling her a devil suggest, Othello's values have been entirely transvalued. He asks Desdemona for her hand, observes that it is moist, and defines it, and her: "For heere's a yong, and sweating Divell heere." He demands the magical handkerchief that he gave her, and when she says that she does not have it with her, announces:

> To loose't, or give't away, were such perdition,
> As nothing else could match.

As Othello finishes his recital of the power of the handkerchief's magic, Desdemona exclaims, "Then would to Heaven, that I had never seene't." When Iago later assures Æmilia (with heavy irony) that Othello is of almost superhuman calm, his example is that Iago saw him remain calm once when the cannon decimated his ranks

> And like the Divell from his very Arme
> Puff't his owne Brother.

Iago exits, and Desdemona is left talking to Æmilia. Desdemona answers Æmilia's suggestion that Othello may be jealous with a proclamation of her absolute innocence: "Alas the day, I never gave him cause"; when Æmilia defines jealousy in terms related to Iago's earlier definition ("It is a Monster / Begot upon it selfe, borne on it selfe"), Desdemona answers, "Heaven keepe the Monster from Othello's mind," and Æmilia adds, "Lady, Amen."

In the first scene of the fourth act, when Iago suggests that even if Desdemona and Cassio lay naked together in bed for an hour or more, they may not have meant any harm, Othello replies:

> Naked in bed (Iago) and not meane harme?
> It is hypocrisie against the Divell:

They that meane vertuously, and yet do so,
The Divell their vertue tempts, and they
    tempt Heaven.

The last words he babbles, before he falls into his
trance, are "O Divell." When Othello revives, to hear
Iago ask if he has hurt his head, he takes it to be
another reference to the horns of cuckoldry, and asks
Iago if he mocks him. Iago's reply is his usual sancti-
monious (and blasphemous) assurance: "I mocke you
not, by Heaven." Iago then offers the provocative com-
fort that millions of men are married to unchaste
women, and, picking up the earlier imagery, adds,
"Oh, 'tis the spight of hell, the Fiends Arch-mock," as
indeed, Iago's own workings are. He concludes the
speech with one of his many covert revelations of his
true identity: "And knowing what I am, I know what
she shallbe." In the following confrontation with Cassio, in which Iago talks of Bianca and the concealed
Othello understands them to be discussing Desdemona, Cassio asks if Iago is telling him the truth, and
Iago assures him (he is of course *not* telling the
truth): "I am a very Villaine else." When Bianca
enters, she curses Cassio with more unconscious
irony, "Let the divell, and his dam haunt you."
Othello, convinced by the scene and the sight of his
magical handkerchief, given to Desdemona, in Cassio's hands and given by Cassio to a whore, goes
"mad" as Iago said he would, and resolves on the
deaths of both Desdemona and Cassio. He is immediately swung the other way by thoughts of what in this

context has to be called Desdemona's sanctity. "Oh she will sing the Savagenesse out of a Beare," he cries out. "And then of so gentle a condition?" he asks himself rhetorically, concluding, "But yet the pitty of it, Iago: oh Iago, the pitty of it Iago." A moment later he is raving: "I will chop her into Messes." Othello's reaction to Iago's suggestion that Desdemona be strangled in the bed she has contaminated, still very much in his world of moral inversion, is "The Justice of it pleases." When Lodovico enters with Desdemona and greets Othello with "Save you worthy Generall" (that is, "God save"), Othello, who in the religious parallel is already eternally damned, answers, "With all my heart Sir." When Desdemona innocently refers to "the love I beare to Cassio," Othello exclaims "Fire, and brimestone." When Desdemona addresses him as "sweete Othello," he calls her "Divell," and, in Theobald's stage direction at least, strikes her. Desdemona answers meekly, "I have not deserv'd this," Lodovico advises, "Make her amends: she weepes," and Othello can only repeat madly, "Oh divell, divell." When Lodovico asks Iago what has come over Othello, Iago answers cryptically, "He's that he is," which is at once his characteristic sort of non-explanation, and in theological terms the fullest possible explanation, in its echo of Iago's own earlier "I am not what I am."

The second scene of the act begins with a conversation between Othello and Æmilia, in which Æmilia assures Othello of Desdemona's absolute integrity in terms that make the religious parallel almost overt.

"She is honest," Æmilia says, "Lay downe my Soule at stake," and continues:

If any wretch have put this in your head,
Let Heaven requit it with the Serpents curse,
For if she be not honest, chaste, and true,
There's no man happy. The purest of their Wives
Is foule as Slander.

(The serpent's curse is God's curse on the serpent in Gen. 3:15, that mankind descended from Eve shall bruise the heads of the serpent's descendants, taken by later Christian interpreters as a prophecy that Eve's descendant Christ would destroy the serpent Satan.) Othello sends Æmilia to fetch Desdemona, and dismisses Æmilia's sacred oath as just an example of her villainy, although he adds, "And yet she'le kneele, and pray: I have seene her do't." Othello then confronts Desdemona in similarly topsy-turvy terms, reversing salvation and damnation. He says:

Come sweare it: damne thy selfe, least being like
one of Heaven, the divells themselves should fear
to ceaze thee. Therefore be double damn'd:
sweare thou art honest.

Desdemona answers, with the absolute assurance of her innocence, "Heaven doth truely know it," to which Othello replies, "Heaven truely knowes, that thou art false as hell." Othello then describes their love as having been the fountain from which he drew his sustenance, and adds bitterly that he may now discard it,

> Or keepe it as a Cesterne, for foule Toades
> To knot and gender in.

"I heere looke grim as hell," he adds. Desdemona asks meekly, "Alas, what ignorant sin have I committed?" and Othello answers: "What commited? / Heaven stoppes the Nose at it." Othello then asks her coarsely, "Are not you a Strumpet?" and Desdemona replies, "No, as I am a Christian." When he repeats more strongly, "What, not a Whore?" she replies with the perfect faith of her *Imitatio Christi*, "No, as I shall be sav'd." Desdemona adds, with absolute charity, "Oh Heaven forgive us," and Othello replies with utter uncharity, calling Æmilia in and addressing her as

> You Mistris,
> That have the office opposite to Saint Peter,
> And keepes the gate of hell.

When Othello departs and leaves them alone together, Æmilia refers to "my Lord," meaning Othello, and Desdemona replies "Who is thy Lord?" to which Æmilia answers, "He that is yours, sweet Lady," which transcends Othello to make it an ambiguous reference to God. When Æmilia has left and reentered with Iago, Iago asks what has come over Othello, and Æmilia shrewdly guesses that Desdemona has been slandered opportunistically by "some eternal Villaine, / Some busie and insinuating Rogue" (Walker convincingly suggests that here, as in two passages he cites from *Hamlet*, "eternal" has been used for "infernal"). Iago answers characteristically, "Fie, there is no such man: it is impossible," and Desdemona answers in her Christlike character, "If any such there be, Heaven pardon him." Æmilia, less charitably and more prophetically, proposes "A halter pardon him: / And hell gnaw his bones." Æmilia adds:

The Moore's abus'd by some most villanous Knave,
Some base notorious Knave, some scurvy Fellow.
Oh Heavens, that such companions thou'd'st unfold.

Desdemona then appeals to Iago for advice about winning back Othello, and in a holy equivalent for Othello's earlier kneeling with Iago in a Satanic pact, kneels in Iago's presence and swears:

> Heere I kneele:
> If ere my will did trespasse 'gainst his Love,
> Either in discourse of thought, or actuall deed
> . . . .
> Comfort forsweare me.

In his edition, Steevens quotes an anonymous comment that the Quartos are right in reading "or thought" rather than "of thought," since Desdemona refers to the three ways of committing sin mentioned in the Catholic Catechisms ("and in our Liturgy," adds Steevens), in thought, word, and deed. Desdemona goes on in the same speech to reject "the worlds Masse of vanitie" as without power to make her sin. Iago has the final word, as Desdemona and Æmilia are leaving, Dame Julian's "all things shall be well," which in this theological context has a wild anti-Christian ring. When Rodorigo enters, Iago promises him "If thou the next night following enjoy not Desdemona, take me from this world with Treacherie, and devise Engines for my life."

In the third scene, Desdemona and Æmilia are left alone after Othello has ordered Desdemona to go instantly to bed. She utters a kind of prayer: "All's one: good Father, how foolish are our minds?" Soon afterwards Desdemona asks Æmilia if she would be unfaithful to her husband, and when the question is turned back on her, answers "No, by this Heavenly light." Æmilia then gives her own cynical answer, in sharp contrast to Desdemona's absolute innocence:

> Nor I neither, by this Heavenly light:
> I might doo't as well i'th'darke.

Desdemona then asks, "Woud'st thou do such a deed for al the world?" and after another cynical reply by Æmilia, answers the question herself, in a formal rejection of the temptation which echoes Christ's rejection of Satan's temptation in the Wilderness. She says:

> Beshrew me, if I would do such a wrong
> For the whole world.

In the first scene of the fifth act, Iago's placing of Rodorigo to assassinate Cassio, his announcement that he profits from any eventuation, discussed above as an example of the stage villain's duplicity and ruthlessness, is more deeply a Satanic revelation. When Othello enters, and concludes that Iago has killed Cassio, he threatens the rest of their demonic commitment in an apostrophe to the absent Desdemona, "your unblest Fate highes." When Iago stabs the wounded Rodorigo to death, the dying man curses him, "O damn'd Iago! O inhumane Dogge!" He is the first person in the play to recognize (in his gut, alas) the full extent of Iago's Satanic nature.

As Iago had entered the scene to do his act of darkness ironically bearing a light, so in the second scene in the act, Othello enters Desdemona's bedroom to do *his* act of darkness bearing a light. In his first soliloquy, "Put out the Light, and then put out the Light," he equates his earthly candle with her heavenly light. He addresses his candle as "thou flaming Minister," which suggests a far more significant light, the sun, which his deed will temporarily extinguish. He continues, in a most powerful statement, "I will kill thee, / And love thee after," which is the fate of Judas. "This sorrow's heavenly," he continues, along the same lines, "It strikes, where it doth love." Desdemona then awakes, and they have the following dialogue:

Othello.	Have you pray'd to night, Desdemon?
Desdemona.	Aye my Lord.
Othello.	If you bethinke your selfe of any Crime
	Unreconcil'd as yet to Heaven, and Grace,
	Solicite for it straight.

. . . .

47

Othello.   I would not kill thy unprepared Spirit,
No, Heavens fore-fend, I would not kill
thy Soule.

. . . .

Desdemona. Then Heaven have mercy on mee.
Othello. Amen, with all my heart.
Desdemona. If you say, I hope you will not kill me.

. . . .

Desdemona. And yet I feare you: for you're fatall
then
When your eyes rowle so.
Why I should feare, I know not,
Since guiltinesse I know not: But yet
I feele I feare.

Many of the themes of Christ's Betrayal and Passion
emerge in this dialogue. Othello says that he would
not kill Desdemona without giving her an opportunity
to confess her sins, although he in fact does precisely
that, but since she is a spotless being without sin, this
makes little difference. He says that he would not kill
her soul, but of course he could not, since her soul will
promptly ascend to Heaven. Desdemona says that she
is guiltless, as befits a being entirely without sin, but
she fears nevertheless, which is reminiscent of Christ's
crying out on the Cross in the Gospels of Matthew
and Mark. Desdemona then continues, full of sanctity: when Othello says "Thou art to dye," she answers, "O Heaven have mercy on me," and adds:

And have you mercy too. I never did
Offend you in my life: never lov'd Cassio,

But with such generall warrantie of Heaven,
As I might love.

Othello, moved, says that she makes him call "A
Murther, which I thought a Sacrifice." Renewed nevertheless in his evil intention, Othello insists that he
must kill her immediately, and when she asks for a
chance to "say one prayer," he answers brutally, "It is
too late," and smothers her. At that moment, Æmilia
enters, crying out:

My Lord, my Lord? What hoa?
My Lord, My Lord.

(The first Quarto assigns the first three "My Lords"
to Desdemona, and this would give Desdemona a fine
Christlike death, but it is unconvincing in context, and
has persuaded only one editor.) Granting that these
are Æmilia's exclamations, they refer to Othello, but
much more significantly, in this theological context, to
God. When Æmilia enters, Othello says to her, of
Desdemona, "I thinke she stirres againe," with its un-
dertones of the Resurrection, and then makes her
identification with Christ explicit in the boldest imagi-
nable fashion. He exclaims:

Oh insupportable! Oh heavy houre!
Me thinkes, it should be now a huge Eclipse
Of Sunne, and Moone; and that th'affrighted Globe
Did yawne at Alteration.

Theobald, in the eighteenth century, naturally caught
the parallel with the Crucifixion. He wrote:

49

Let the Poet account for the profanation, if he
has committed any; but it is very obvious to me
his allusion is grounded on a certain *solemn* cir-
cumstance, when *darkness* is said to have *cov-
ered the whole face of the land*; when *rocks* were
rent; and *graves opened*.

Desdemona then briefly revives, or returns from the
dead, to proclaim "O falsely, falsely murder'd" and "A
guiltlesse death, I dye." When Æmilia asks who
killed her, she answers, with Christ's acknowledg-
ment that he has chosen his own fate and Christ's perfect forgiveness of its agents:

> No body: I my selfe, farewell:
> Commend me to my kinde Lord: oh farewell.

("Lord" here is again God the Father as well as
Othello.) Othello's reaction to this exoneration and
forgiveness, which is strong enough to overcome
death, is truly savage. He says:

> She's like a Liar gone to burning hell,
> 'Twas I that kill'd her.

Æmilia's answer restores the values that Othello has
transvalued. She says, "Oh the more Angell she, and
you the blacker Divell." When he makes further
charges, she repeats, "Thou do'st bely her, and thou
art a divell." When he then charges, "She was false as
water" (which Dr. Johnson shrewdly interpreted to
mean "As water that will support no weight") Æmilia
answers "Oh she was heavenly true," with its lovely

suggestion that water will support the weight of the
heavenly true. If he did not commit his murder "upon
just grounds," Othello says, "O, I were damn'd beneath all depth in hell," and since he surely did not, he
assuredly is, as Judas is believed to be. When Othello
finally succeeds in getting through Æmilia's shock
and incredulity the realization that it was *her* husband
who gave him the evidence against Desdemona,
Æmilia curses Iago in similar terms of eternal damnation. She says:

> If he say so, may his pernicious Soule
> Rot halfe a graine a day: he lyes to'th'heart.

As Æmilia cries out "Murther, Murther," Iago enters
with Montano and Gratiano. She immediately charges
him with responsibility for Othello's deed:

Oh, are you come, Iago: you have done well,
That men must lay their Murthers on your necke.

When he admits that he told Othello that Desdemona
was false, she further indicts him in his character as
the Prince of Lies:

> You told a Lye an odious damned Lye:
> Upon my Soule, a Lye; a wicked Lye.

Æmilia then similarly charges Othello with the sort
of betrayal which fits his role as a Judas:

> Nay, lay thee downe, and roare:
> For thou hast kill'd the sweetest innocent,
> That ere did lift up eye.

51

Hearing more of Iago's charges against Desdemona, Æmilia cries out "Oh Heaven! oh heavenly Powres!" and when Iago tries to quiet her, continues:

Let Heaven, and Men, and Divels, let them all,
All, all, crie shame against me, yet Ile speake.

As Æmilia continues to reveal Iago's depravity, he charges that she lies, and she swears again, "By Heaven I do not." By this time Iago has drawn his dagger against Æmilia, and as Othello, finally convinced, runs at Iago, Iago stabs Æmilia to death and escapes. Dying, she implores, "Oh lay me by my Mistris side." Her last words include what I think is the most beautiful single line in the play: "Moore, she was chaste: She lov'd thee, cruell Moore," a truly Christlike description of Desdemona, followed by Æmilia's final assurance, "So come my Soule to blisse, as I speake true." (On the basis of her role in this scene, from Desdemona's death to Æmilia's own sacrificial death, one may identify Æmilia's role in the Christian parallel: weak and sinful woman that she is, she is emblematic of the repentant Good Thief Dismas and her own salvation is assured.) Othello then makes the first of his confessional speeches that constitute the play's final movement. It sharply supports both Desdemona's assurance of Heaven and her nature as a figuration of the Christ. He proclaims over her corpse:

when we shall meete at compt,
This looke of thine will hurle my Soule from Heaven,
And Fiends will snatch at it.

"Compt" is the accounting, the Last Judgment, and in this most poignant vision, Desdemona will not only be in Heaven but will be judging in Heaven, and dispatching Othello's soul to hell. He goes on to sentence himself similarly in advance, crying out:

> Whip me ye Divels,
> From the possession of this Heavenly sight:
> Blow me about in windes, roast me in Sulphure,
> Wash me in steepe-downe gulfes of Liquid fire.

(This is what theologians call "the repentance of Judas," unique in that it is repentance without hope of God's mercy or redemption.) Iago is then brought in under guard, and Othello says:

> I look down toward his feet; but that's a Fable,
> If that thou bee'st a Divell, I cannot kill thee.

Othello runs at him with his sword and succeeds in wounding him, and Iago says, with open Satanic arrogance, "I bleed Sir, but not kill'd"—he *is* a devil, then. Disarmed and restrained, Othello then asks Cassio:

> Will you, I pray, demand that demy-Divell,
> Why he hath thus ensnar'd my Soule and Body.

Iago's answer is again truly Satanic. He says:

> Demand me nothing: what you know, you know:
> From this time forth, I never will speake word.

Lodovico then asks, somewhat absurdly, "What? not to pray?" and Gratiano says, with easy assurance, "Torments will ope your lips"; but we know, as Swin-

2. *Theological Criticism*

burne said (see below, p. 56) that, indomitable in evil, Iago, as he says, never again will speak word. Lodovico then sentences Iago to torture. The identification with Judas betraying Christ is made openly in a simile or ritual formula in Othello's final speech before he kills himself in despair (as Judas does). He identifies himself as

> one, whose hand
> (Like the base Judean) threw a Pearle away
> Richer then all his Tribe:

"The base Judean" is of course Judas, rejecting the Savior, a pearl more precious than all the Law and the Prophets.* Finally, in his last words before he dies, Othello says "I kist thee, ere I kill'd thee," and the analogy is complete. The last speech in the play is Lodovico's, identifying Iago as "More fell then Anguish, Hunger, or the Sea" and as "this hellish villaine."

---

* We can see a contemporary sense of this contrast in Lancelot Andrewes' "Sermon 5 of the Nativitie," preached at Christmas, 1610, within a few years of the composition of *Othello*. (It also furnishes a useful example of contemporary typology or pre-figuration.) Andrewes writes:

> For many *Saviours* had been borne, many had God sent them, that at divers times had set them free from divers dangers of their enemies, *Moses* from the *Egyptians*, *Joshua* from the *Canaanites*, *Gideon* from the *Midianites*, *Jepthe* from the *Ammonites*, *Samson* from the *Philistims*. And indeed, the whole storie of the Bible is nothing else but a Calender of *Saviours* that God from time to time still stirred them up.
>
> But these all were but pettie *Saviours*, there was one yet behind, that was worth them all . . . . *a Saviour which was Christ.*

* * *

This parallel of the play with Judas' betrayal of Christ has had a curious history in scholarship and criticism. Most editors have been unable to make any sense out of "the base Judean" (which requires a Biblical knowledge which most of them have not had, the knowledge that Judas Iscariot, whose name means something like "Jew Traitor," was the only Judean among the Apostles, the other eleven being Galileans). Consequently they have obscured the parallel for readers by reprinting the misprint "base Indian" of the Quartos rather than the "base Iudean" of the First Folio, and gone hunting stories about Indian pearl tossers.

Many critics have noticed, if not that Desdemona is a figuration of the Christ—although Guy Boas did, half a century ago—at least that she is a being of perfect innocence and virtue out of some Prelapsarian world (see Br. Nicholson above): in Mrs. Jameson's words, "a victim consecrated from the first, 'an offering without blemish.'" Heilman points out that her refusal to sin "For the whole world" is "another reminiscence of the Christian myth."

Many other scholars and critics (along with most of the characters in the last scene of *Othello*) have observed that if Iago is not a figuration of Satan, he is at least devilish and demonic in the extreme. Bradley identified him with Mephistopheles. In *Shakespeare Studies* (1927) E. E. Stoll observes: "Iago is the

55

great devil of the seventeenth century as Goethe's Mephistopheles is of the nineteenth," and in *Shakespeare and Other Masters* (1940) he lists other critics who share his reading. Maud Bodkin deals with Iago as an example of the devil archetype in *Archetypal Patterns in Poetry* (1934). In *Shakespeare's Use of Learning* (1953), Virgil Whitaker observes: "Iago's character is founded upon pride or self-love, the very source of all sin." G. R. Elliott's *Flaming Minister* (1953) traces the theme of "divinity of hell" through the play. Roy Battenhouse's "Shakespearean Tragedy: A Christian Approach" (1957), reprinted in Rabkin's *Approaches to Shakespeare*, sees Iago as emblematic of Satan and relates him to Othello as a figure who is emblematic of Judas. Three readings familiar to me are particularly interesting in that they define Iago's nature in terms which are essentially theological. The first of them is Coleridge's, whose final interpretation falls roughly midway between the Satanic and the Machiavellian (for convenience, it will be discussed later, in connection with the latter), but who called Iago "next to devil and only not quite devil." The second is Swinburne's, who wrote:

Iago has within him a sense or conscience of power incomparable: and this power shall not be left, in Hamlet's phrase, 'to fust in him unused.' A genuine and thorough capacity for human lust or hate would diminish and degrade the supremacy of his evil. He is almost as far

above or beyond vice as he is beneath or beyond
virtue. And this it is which makes him impreg-
nable and invulnerable. When once he has said
it, we know as well as he that henceforth he
never will speak word. We could smile almost as
we can see him to have smiled at Gratiano's most
ignorant and empty threat, being well assured
that torments will in no wise ope his lips; that
as surely and as truly as ever did the tortured
philosopher before him, he might have told his
tormenters that they did but bruise the coating,
batter the crust, or break the shell of Iago. Could
we imagine a far other lost spirit than Farinata
degli Uberti's endowed with Farinata's might of
will, and transferred from the sepulchres of fire
to the dykes of Malebolge, we might conceive
something of Iago's attitude in hell,—of his un-
alterable and indomitable posture for all eternity.

The third such reading is that of Robert B. Heilman
in *Magic in the Web*. By 1956 he had not only worked
out the whole Christian triad of the play, Desdemona-
Othello-Iago as Christ-Judas-Satan, come out for the
"base Judean" reading (at least for the purposes of
this interpretation), and observed Iago's characteristic
Satanic working "by corrupting a virtue," but had
even made some literary parallels of great fertility and
suggestiveness. Heilman identifies the Satanic aspect
of Iago (always insisting that in another aspect Iago
is a human being) with Milton's Satan in *Paradise*

Lost and (following F. O. Matthiessen in *American Renaissance*) with Melville's Claggart in "Billy Budd." He shows the analogy with Milton's Satan in everything from basic stance to details of language; and says, of the latter analogy:

> Melville might be portraying Iago when he draws on the concept of "natural depravity" and lists, among the characteristics of Claggart, respectability, the use of reason as "an ambidexter implement for effecting the irrational," "uncommon prudence," the use of "retaliation . . . in monstrous disproportion to the supposed offense," the fact that he "justified animosity into a sort of retributive righteousness," the "monomania in the man." Iago also has the sense of personal antithesis which is implicitly present in Claggart: "If Cassio do remain, / He hath a daily beauty in his life / That makes me ugly" (5.1.18–20). The perception to which every villain with a mind is doomed is here used by Shakespeare to set forth in precise words that aspect of evil which he has already set forth in action, namely, its springing into full life at the implicit challenge of a counterexistence. Dormant evil is awakened by the juxtaposition of conspicuous good (Claggart by the arrival of Budd)—duplicity by integrity, mendacity by truthfulness, hate by love. Iago's hatred of Othello is activated when Othello, as successful lover, inclines to

love all the world, and of Cassio when he is deep in a reciprocal friendly love with both Othello and Desdemona.

The realization that Othello had the role of Judas in the myth, however, proved too incongruous to come into print for more than two centuries, and then it was another quarter century before it could be taken seriously. In 1841, Knight wrote on the "base Judean": "To show how far conjecture may be carried, we may mention that a correspondent wishes to impress upon us that the allusion was to Judas Iscariot." In 1885, Halliwell observed:

> The epithet 'base' appears to support 'Iudean,' which, if correct, I cannot but think, notwithstanding that the idea has been ridiculed, refers to Judas Iscariot . . . . Once before in this Scene, Othello's agonized thoughts had turned for a fit comparison to that dread time when the affrighted globe yawned and darkness covered the face of the earth.

Furness reprints this in his *Variorum* with the comment, "I have reserved Halliwell's opinion to the last, because, to me, it gives the true explanation." Since then, despite this solid authority, most of the editors have continued to prefer "Indian" (although the *Pléiade* has "*Juif infame*"), but there has been a small body of support for the obviously correct First Folio reading. Richmond Noble's book, *Shakespeare's Bibli-*

cal Knowledge (1935), argues that "the base Judean" is Judas ("Just as Judas threw away his Saviour, the most precious possession of his Tribe, so he [Othello] destroyed what had been his most precious blessing"), and further identifies the pearl with the "pearl of great price" in Matthew 13:46, the Kingdom of Heaven. Paul N. Siegel, in *Shakespearean Tragedy and the Elizabethan Compromise* (1957), works out the parallel in elaborate and convincing detail, apparently independently of Heilman. If these writers augur a breed of modern Shakespeare scholars who know the Bible equally well, we can expect the base Indian to vanish from future editions.

[3]

THE APPROACH HERE is symbolic action criticism, seeing Iago as an image of the artist or playwright, in his criminal aspect; as Kenneth Burke, who developed this approach as one facet of his critical method, says in his 1951 article on *Othello*, Iago is "an ominous caricature of the playwright's own methods." For effective contrast, I am matching him against his antithesis, Prospero in *The Tempest*, a caricature of the benign artist.

In this perspective, what motivates Iago is the playwright's delight in creating illusion and manipulating people by his powers of deception. For Shakespeare, Iago is a merciless self-portrait as artist-criminal (the type which so fascinated Thomas Mann in such characters as Cippola and Adrian Leverkühn), and a therapeutic symbolic action of purging away the guilt of Shakespeare's Faustian craft.

As a metaphor for the artist, Iago is the master of lies and deceit, his aim the creation of discord and evil, as Prospero is the antithetical metaphor, the master of magic illusion, the creator of harmony and good. *Othello* is unintelligible unless one assumes that we should not necessarily believe Iago under any

61

circumstances, even when he is addressing the audience or speaking in an aside (which contradicts the theatrical convention, and Shakespeare's own habitual practice, whereby such soliloquies and asides are always honest). Here the basic advice came from Knight in 1841. His views are given by Furness in his *Variorum:*

> Knight maintains that we can gather no trustworthy information from anything which Iago may say on this or on any subject (wherein the present editor agrees with him). 'It is not to be forgotten that Iago, throughout the whole course of his extraordinary character, is represented as utterly regardless of the differences between truth and falsehood. The most absolute lie,— the half lie,—the truth in the way of telling it distorted into a lie, are the instruments with which Iago constantly works.'

We can see a perfect miniature of the artist as liar in Iago's treatment of Cassio. He envies him, hates him, entices him into disgrace, then uses him to get Desdemona killed and tries through both Rodorigo's efforts and his own to kill him too. His public remarks about Cassio are of quite another tenor. Iago replies to Montano's suggestion that Iago tell Othello that Cassio is an untrustworthy drunkard:

> Not I, for this faire Island,
> I do love Cassio well: and would do much
> To cure him of this evill.

When Cassio wounds Montano, and Othello asks who began the quarrel, Iago replies similarly:

I had rather have this tongue cut from my mouth,
Then it should do offense to Michaell Cassio.

Without formally saying that Cassio began the quarrel, Iago then admits that he heard Cassio "high in oath," adding sanctimoniously, "Which till to night / I nere might say before." He then goes on to implicate Cassio further, in the guise of excusing him:

But Men are Men: The best sometimes forget,
Though Cassio did some little wrong to him,
As men in rage strike those that wish them best,
Yet surely Cassio, I beleeve receiv'd
From him that fled, some strange Indignitie,
Which patience could not passe.

Othello's inevitable reaction to this is to praise Iago's honesty and love, and to discharge Cassio offhand. As soon as Iago is alone with the disgraced Cassio, he adds the final lie: "And good Lieutenant, I thinke, you thinke I love you" (with all the fine ambiguity of the second "think").

This rather simple-minded technique of the artist, the flat untruth, becomes much more sophisticated when Iago pursues his main plot against Desdemona and Othello. Here he tells lies and part-lies enough, surely, but his main reliance is on the much more effective power of suggestion. He first practices it on Cassio, when the latter arrives on Cyprus with Othello and Desdemona. To each of Cassio's innocent, even reverential, praises of their general's new wife, Iago replies with a sly insinuation that she is lecherous and thus available. "She is sport for Jove," he says, "And Ile warrant her, full of Game"; "What an eye she ha's? / Methinkes it sounds a parley to provocation"; and he concludes, "Well: happinesse to their Sheetes." This is merely a foretaste of Iago's great rhetorical triumphs of Act III, scene 3, when he first arouses Othello's suspicions by the most economical of means, the smallest whispers of hints, as in the following exchange, as Othello and Iago see Cassio taking leave of Desdemona:

Iago. Hah? I like not that.
Othello. What dost thou say?
Iago. Nothing my Lord; or if—I know not what.
Othello. Was not that Cassio parted from my wife?
Iago. Cassio my Lord? No sure, I cannot thinke it
That he would steale away so guilty-like,
Seeing your comming

Lewes comments on this technique: "It is one of the artifices of Iago to make his victim draw every conclusion from premises which are put before him, so that, in the event of detection, he can say, 'I said nothing, I made no accusation.' " With masterly art, Iago says less and less to greater and greater effect as the scene develops, so that later, when Othello asks, "Is he not honest?" we get this exchange:

Iago. Honest, my Lord?
Othello. Honest? Aye, Honest.

Iago.	My Lord, for ought I know.
Othello.	What do'st thou thinke?
Iago.	Thinke, my Lord?
Othello.	Thinke, my Lord? Alas, thou ecchos't me;
	As if there were some Monster in thy thought
	Too hideous to be shewne.

Othello continues: "As if thou hadd'st shut up in thy Braine / Some horrible Conceite." He further explains:

> Therefore these stops of thine, fright me the more:
> For such things in a false disloyall Knave
> Are trickes of Custome: but in a man that's just,
> They're close dilations, working from the heart,
> That Passion cannot rule.

Iago then gives Othello a little classic of artistic suggestion-in-non-suggestion. Here is the dialogue:

Iago.	For Michael Cassio,
	I dare be sworn, I thinke that he is honest.
Othello.	I thinke so too.
Iago.	Men should be what they seeme,
	Or those that be not, would they might seeme none.
Othello.	Certaine, men should be what they seeme.
Iago.	Why then I thinke Cassio's an honest man.

By this time, as we can see, Othello has become little more than an assenting lump. Later, in the first scene of the fourth act, he has sunk so far that he as-

sumes Iago's earlier role of echo. When Iago is about
to conjure up his gross vision of Desdemona and Cassio naked in bed together, he begins the scene, "Will
you thinke so?" and Othello echoes tonelessly,
"Thinke so, Iago?" Iago's final triumph in the scene,
along these lines, is a perfect suggestion-non-
suggestion by pun. Othello asks him what Cassio confessed to him:

Othello. What hath he said?
Iago. Why, that he did: I know not what he did.
Othello. What? What?
Iago. Lye.
Othello. With her?
Iago. With her? On her: what you will.
Othello. Lye with her? lye on her? We say lye on her when they be-lye-her. Lye with her: that's fullsome:

Othello then goes on for six more lines of raving and
babbling, and falls into his trance.

The shrewdest part of Iago's technique of artistic
suggestion is that each time he succeeds in heating
Othello to a violent passion, he then cools him with a
dash of cold water, as in the old process for tempering
fine sword blades. When Othello cries "O monstrous!
monstrous!" after hearing Cassio's non-dream, Iago
cautions, "Nay, this was but his Dreame." When
Othello goes on to threaten "Ile teare her all to
peeces," Iago again restrains him, "Nay yet be wise;

yet we see nothing done, / She may be honest yet."
When Othello threatens "blacke vengeance, from the
hollow hell," Iago says soothingly, "Yet be content."
When, finally, Othello cries "O blood, blood, blood,"
Iago is like a good marriage counselor: "Patience I
say: your minde may change." In the terrible scene
where they kneel together in a monstrous pact, Iago
agrees without qualm to murder Cassio, adding
lamely, "But let her live." In the final great seduction
scene, Act IV, scene 1, after Othello has been shown
what he takes to be Cassio boasting of his intimacy
with Desdemona, he threatens terrible violence to
Cassio again, and Iago says benignly, "Nay, you must
forget that," and, when Othello pronounces a comparable death sentence on Desdemona, he adds piously,
"Nay, that's not your way." What makes all this artistic is Iago's perfect command of his medium and his
audience, his perfect control of the degrees of excita-
tion and restraint, and his consummate sense of pace.

Since one of Iago's major techniques is dramatization, he is not only a type of the artist as malign, but a
caricature of the playwright himself. His setting up of
the false Cassio show is a play-within-the-play not unlike Hamlet's. He tells Othello:

> Do but encave your selfe,
> And marke the Fleeres, the Gybes, and notable Scornes
> That dwell in every Region of his face.
> For I will make him tell the Tale anew;
> Where, how, how oft, how long ago, and when

He hath, and is againe to cope your wife.
I say, but marke his gesture:

("Cope" is "cover.") Iago's later horrible suggestion
that Desdemona be killed in the bed she has contaminated is the dramatist's artful fitting of action to scene,
what Burke calls the "scene-act ratio," here a monstrous caricature of dramatic propriety. His setting up
of Rodorigo to assassinate Cassio (or the reverse, or
both, for all he cares) is another clear dramatization,
a deadly play, within the deadlier play of promoting
the murder of Desdemona, within the ultimate deadly
play, the tragedy of *Othello*.

As a masterly dramatist (as Shakespeare, that
is) Iago uses whatever ingredients come to hand.
When he makes his first major effort to undermine
Othello's faith in Desdemona's fidelity, he uses her deceit of her father as an argument, cruelly harvesting
what Brabantio had spitefully planted. Iago says:

She did deceive her Father, marrying you,
And when she seem'd to shake, and feare your lookes,
She lov'd them most.

He uses with equal cruelty and ingenuity Othello's
doubts about his own desirability as a Moor, observing:

Not to affect many proposed Matches
Of her owne Clime, Complexion, and Degree,
Whereto we see in all things, Nature tends:

68

Foh, one may smel in such, a will most ranke,
Foule disproportions, Thoughts unnaturall.

In the last act, when Bianca appears on the scene with
Rodorigo lying dead and Cassio wounded, Iago takes
the same lightning advantage of her accidental appearance to try to implicate her, asking all to observe
the damning evidence of "the gastnesse of her eye,"
and adding sententiously, "Nay, guiltinesse will
speake / Though tongues were out of use."

Beyond that, Iago manipulates people as a dramatist does, from his introductory gulling of Rodorigo,
through his advising Cassio and Desdemona, to his
final manipulation of Othello to kill Desdemona and
thus, inevitably, himself. More than any of these, Iago
is a type of the dramatist in the fact (as he keeps telling his dupes and the audience) that he needs time for
things to germinate. Iago promises Rodorigo in the
first act, "There are many Events in the Wombe of
Time, which wilbe delivered." In the next act, when
Desdemona asks him to improvise verses, Iago uses
the same gestation-and-birth metaphor, but now talks
openly of himself in artistic terms. He says:

> I am about it, but indeed my invention comes
> from my pate, as Birdlyme do's from Freeze, it
> pluckes out Braines and all. But my Muse la-
> bours, and thus she is deliver'd.

At the end of the act, when Iago is stalling Rodorigo,
he tells him what is surely a basic truth about play-

wrights (at least of the Iago, if not of the Prospero, sort):

Thou know'st we worke by Wit, and not by Witch-
 craft
And Wit depends on dilatory time:

As a type of the artist, Iago is a specialist in creating illusion. He creates the illusion that he is loyal
and effective to Rodorigo, that he is honest and loving
to Othello, that he is a reliable adviser and friend to
Cassio, and that he is deeply sympathetic to Desdemona. In a soliloquy to the audience in Act III, scene
3, he explains, in connection with his plan for planting
the handkerchief in Cassio's lodging, the nature of the
illusionist's art:

> Trifles light as ayre,
> Are to the jealious, confirmations strong,
> As proofes of holy Writ.

When Othello, still full of doubt, warns him sternly
later in the same scene:

> Villaine, be sure thou prove my Love a Whore;
> Be sure of it: Give me the Occular proofe,

Iago, who of course cannot give *proof*, as the illusionist cannot, offers to provide him with the artist's sub-
stitute, the illusion he can create. Iago says:

> If imputation, and strong circumstances,
> Which leade directly to the doore of Truth,
> Will give you satisfaction, you might have't.

As a special sort of artist, the criminal or malign type, Iago uses his gifts to bring about general calamity (here the contrast with Prospero's transformations of the malign into something "rich and strange" is most marked). Iago tells the audience that he will win Othello's thanks, love, and reward:

> For making him egregiously an Asse,
> And practising upon his peace, and quiet,
> Even to madnesse.

His plan to use Desdemona as a means of general enmeshing, quoted earlier as an example of Satanism, is just as obviously an aesthetic technique (like Penelope's web and all the related metaphors of catching prey in the *Odyssey*, or Clytemnestra's net and all *its* related metaphors of entrapment in the *Agamemnon*). Iago says:

> So will I turne her vertue into pitch,
> And out of her owne goodnesse make the Net,
> That shall en-mash them all.

In another soliloquy, in Act III, scene 3, as Othello enters, Iago threatens to afflict him with the sort of unease that tragic art characteristically produces:

> Not Poppy, nor Mandragora,
> Nor all the drowsie Syrrups of the world
> Shall ever medicine thee to that sweete sleepe
> Which thou owd'st yesterday.

71

The result of Iago's venture in playwriting is to litter the stage with almost as many corpses as Hamlet's similar enterprise: Rodorigo, Desdemona, Æmilia, and Othello. In the first scene of the first act, he directs Rodorigo, in regard to Brabantio, to "poyson his delight." Shakespeare's play is precisely such an action on the audience, setting up the beautiful and moving love of Othello and Desdemona, then quickly turning it so painful that we can hardly bear it (even if we accept that there is an ultimate Aristotelian pleasure in this therapeutic catharsis).

Beyond all these techniques, Iago is visibly a type of the artist in his style and manner. When he says, in Act I, scene 1, that he pretends to follow Othello loyally "for my peculiar end," it is ultimately the artist's peculiar end, to create his own aesthetic artifact (however malign and criminal it may be). When Othello praises Iago in Act III, scene 3, for his honesty, and adds:

> And knowes all Quantities with a learn'd Spirit
> Of humane dealings,

Lettsom seems only wrong about the "unconsciously" when he notes "In this passage the poet has unconsciously described himself." In the first scene of the second act, this professionalism is most visible in the rhyming scene with Desdemona. Urged, perhaps even forced (if his protestations can be believed) to improvise on set topics, he improvises quickly and in a masterly fashion, giving Desdemona more than she bargained for in the slurs on women and the final brilliant, and perfectly-timed, deflation. It is a dazzling display of artistry—William Shakespeare's artistry. Iago here is a paradigm for Shakespeare: versifying on demand, but versifying better than they know, and a "scald rimer" indeed.*

Iago similarly shows us Shakespeare's equal brilliance in improvising dramatic action. When trying to decide on his plot at the end of the first act, he asks himself "How? How? Let's see," then sketches out his plan with Othello's natural vulnerability to it, and concludes (in the metaphor of gestation discussed earlier), "I have't: it is engendred." These quick musings reproduce the playwright's stages of finding his dramatic action, shaping a character to make the action credible, and realizing that it will work theatrically. Iago shows the same improvisatory gift, in a trivial example, in the conversation with Æmilia in Act III, scene 3, when he coarsely dismisses her "I have a thing for you" with "It is a common thing—," and when she asks "Hah?" immediately replies, "To have a foolish wife." In Act I, scene 1, we see Iago displaying Shakespeare's characteristic choice of speech as we know it in such Sonnets as 109 and 110. Iago's first words in the play, to Rodorigo, are:

But you'l not heare me. If ever I did dream
Of such a matter, abhorre me.

* Stoll observes in *Shakespeare and Other Masters:* "the villain derives a perilous pleasure out of skating on thin ice and almost giving himself away," and Heilman remarks: "For Iago, naming of what he is doing heightens the pleasure of the risky game."

Assuring Rodorigo that he hates Othello, Iago continues, "Despise me / If I do not." Cleopatra regains Anthony's trust by similar rhetoric: it is the use of negative magic as an earnest. Later in the scene, when Brabantio charges "Thou art a Villaine," Iago answers, in another form of Shakespearian rhetoric, the deflation of expectations, "You are a Senator." At other times Iago uses perfect simple eloquence, as in Act III, scene 3, when Othello complains miserably that his unhappiness comes from the canker of knowledge of Desdemona's infidelity, and Iago answers, in a tone of quiet sympathy almost unique for him, "I am sorry to heare this." His much more typical literary style comes in his next-to-last speech in the play (before the final one proclaiming that he will never speak more), in which he shows a kind of ultimate bravado and wit after Othello has wounded him, observing defiantly, "I bleed Sir, but not kill'd."

Finally, Iago sometimes seems to comment obliquely on Shakespeare's own social role and status. In Act I, scene 1, his "I know my price" has some of the bitterness of the commercial writer; when Iago says, in the heart-on-the-sleeve speech quoted earlier, that he dissembles "for my peculiar end," in an autobiographical context it might suggest Shakespeare's own self-justification in regard to his social climb that led to his purchase of New Place and a coat of arms, and his eventual retirement to Stratford as a gentleman. Iago's reluctance to improvise verses for Desdemona (if not feigned) suggests some of the same ambivalence about his art. We see a similar reluctance, like the playwright's guilt about the effects of his play, early in Iago's seduction of Othello in Act III, scene 3, when Iago says, in a tone that seems closer to honest reluctance than he reveals at any other time:

> It were not for your quiet, nor your good,
> Nor for my Manhood, Honesty, and Wisedome,
> To let you know my thoughts.

Romanticism's cult of the Byronic poet taught the nineteenth century that Iago was a type of the artist. Hazlitt wrote in 1817, "He is an amateur of tragedy in real life; and instead of employing his invention on imaginary characters or long-forgotten incidents, he takes the bolder and more desperate course of getting up his plot at home, casts the principal parts among his nearest friends and connections, and rehearses it in downright earnest with steady nerves and unabated resolution." Hudson in 1881 commented on Iago's "pride of intellect, or lust of the brain, which exults above all things in being able to make himself and others pass for just the reverse of what they are; that is, in being an over-match for truth and Nature themselves." Swinburne called Iago (with a most peculiar choice of adjective) "an inarticulate poet."

In our century, the chief spokesman for this view of Iago as artist has been A. C. Bradley. He writes in *Shakespearean Tragedy:* "But Iago, finally, is not simply a man of action; he is an artist. His action is a plot, the intricate plot of a drama, and in the conception and execution of it he experiences the tension and the joy of artistic creation . . . Shakespeare put a good deal of himself into Iago." In another place Bradley notes as "a curious point of technique" that Iago's "soliloquies . . . read almost like explanations offered to the audience" by the playwright himself. Harley Granville-Barker, in *Prefaces to Shakespeare* (1947), has a long discussion of Iago as "artist." In *The Disciplines of Criticism*, edited by Peter Demetz and others (1969), A. Bartlett Giamatti gives us a generalization about the Renaissance artist as a power figure which underlies the whole problem of Iago as a guilty self-portrait. Giamatti writes: "In the Renaissance, the power to manipulate words carried awesome responsibilities. As words could create, imitate, and ennoble, they could also falsify and deceive, projecting illusions which bore no necessary relation to actuality."

Finally, since symbolic action criticism of this sort was created as a strand of Kenneth Burke's method, we may properly end on some observations in Burke's own analysis of the play, "*Othello:* An Essay to Illustrate a Method" in *Perspectives by Incongruity*. This essay not only treats the play, in one aspect, as a "ritual of riddance" for Shakespeare as well as for the audience, but compares it with *The Tempest*, "since Prospero is even more influential than Iago in overseeing the development of the plot."

* * *

Prospero is a radically antithetical portrait of the artist, as benign magician, creating only harmony and concord. He is almost godlike in his creative abilities, his control of magical powers, and his prescience. When Ferdinand finally hears an example of the beautiful music that is emblematic of the island and the play, Ariel invisible playing and singing "Come Unto These Yellow Sands," he comments:

Where shold this Musick be? I'th aire, or th'earth?
It sounds no more: and sure it waytes upon
Some God o'th'Iland.

In Act I, scene 2, when Ferdinand encounters Prospero, who as the god of the island (for his peculiar end) insults and threatens him, Ferdinand draws his sword, and is immediately charmed immobile—he admits ruefully, "My spirits, as in a dreame, are all bound up." In the first scene of the next act, Prospero similarly charms Alonso and Gonzalo asleep, so that Anthonio and Sebastian can work out their treacherous and murderous plot. As the plot reaches the sticking-point, Prospero's prescience sends Ariel to awaken the prospective victims with his characteristic music and song. Ariel says to Gonzalo:

My Master through his Art foresees the danger
That you (his friend) are in, and sends me forth
(For else his project dies) to keep them living.

When Caliban first encounters Stephano, and sees him shaking from drink, his automatic comment is "Now Prosper workes upon thee."

Prospero concludes the first scene of the third act with the sort of soliloquy of his intentions to the audience which contrasts so radically with Iago's soliloquies. He announces:

> Ile to my booke,
> For yet ere supper time, must I performe
> Much businesse appertaining.

The essence of Prospero's power lies in his book or books, as befits an artist. When Caliban offers to lead Sebastian to Prospero asleep, so that Sebastian can knock a nail into his head, the invisible Ariel contradicts him sharply: "Thou liest, thou canst not." In Caliban's view at least, all that could prevent his scheme is Prospero's magic books, and he warns Sebastian "there thou maist braine him, / Having first seiz'd his bookes," and adds:

> Remember
> First to possesse his Bookes; for without them
> Hee's but a Sot, as I am; nor hath not
> One Spirit to command: they all do hate him
> As rootedly as I. Burne but his bookes.

To open the last act, Prospero enters, garbed in his magic robes, and proclaims, as an imaginative playwright might,

Now do's my Project gather to a head:
My charmes cracke not: my Spirits obey.

Prospero claims (and may have) control of all
sorts of supernatural powers, but as we observe his
magical arts in the play, they are mainly contrived by
Ariel, an airy and lyric spirit whom he summons and
directs frequently. He begins in the second scene of
the first act by reminding Ariel, who has protested his
hard labors, of the plight in which he found him, im-
prisoned in a cloven pine by the witch Sycorax for
twelve years. During that period Ariel was not exactly
the fount of harmonious music he has since become;
Prospero reminds him: "thy grones / Did make
wolves howle, and penetrate the breasts / Of ever-
angry Beares." He then recalls Ariel to his indebted-
ness: "it was mine Art, / When I arriv'd, and heard
thee, that made gape / The Pyne, and let thee out."
Ariel properly thanks him, and shows no further sign
of rebellion, but Prospero goes on to add the only
threat that he makes to Ariel in the course of the play:

If thou more murmur'st, I will rend an Oake
And peg-thee in his knotty entrailes, till
Thou has howl'd away twelve winters.

(That is, Prospero could be as wicked as the witch
Sycorax, or the criminal Iago, if he so wished.) Ariel
then asks pardon and agrees willingly to serve, and
from that moment on Prospero's treatment of him is
entirely different. He immediately promises release:

79

Doe so: and after two daies
I will discharge thee.

As Ariel succeeds at his duties, Prospero repeats the
promise by way of congratulation: "Spirit, fine spirit,
Ile free thee / Within two dayes for this." After Ariel
has executed another complex magical feat, Prospero
praises the excellence of his performance, and then
seems to credit in addition an army of lesser anonymous spirits:

                              so with good life,
And observation strange, my meaner ministers
Their severall kindes have done: my high charmes
     work.

In the fourth act, when Prospero again summons
and instructs Ariel, Ariel agrees to perform the tasks
in a trice, and then asks, as a child might, "Doe you
love me Master?" to which Prospero promptly replies,
"Dearely, my delicate Ariell." In his last words in the
act, Prospero reassures Ariel

    Shortly shall all my labours end, and thou
    Shalt have the ayre at freedome:

As they begin the last act, Ariel reminds Prospero
that it is the day "You said our worke should cease," to
which Prospero replies, "I did say so, / When first I
rais'd the Tempest." As Ariel helps dress Prospero in
his Duke of Milan costume, singing his lovely
"Where the Bee Sucks, There Suck I," Prospero

praises him and accepts his imminent departure with genuine regret:

Why that's my dainty Ariell: I shall misse
Thee, but yet thou shalt have freedome: so, so, so.

Ariel's reaction is to become even more airy, and to promise to execute his next-to-last task by being even more magically quick than before:

I drinke the aire before me, and returne
Or ere your pulse twice beate.

That done, Prospero praises him as "My tricksey Spirit," and when Ariel asks for praise, "Was't well done?" Prospero answers, "Bravely (my diligence) thou shalt be free." Finally, in his words that conclude the play (except for the perhaps spurious Epilogue), Prospero promises the departing Alonso and company calm seas and winds, and turns finally to Ariel:

My Ariel; chicke
That is thy charge: Then to the Elements
Be free, and fare thou well:

It is obvious, in this portrait of the artist as benign magician, or glorified self-portrait of Shakespeare, that Ariel is his lyric gift: wonderfully capable, beloved, but ultimately transient. In the same perspective, Caliban is the inner depths, from which Shakespeare draws his darker powers, but here the relation is almost entirely coercive, and sometimes actively hostile. When Prospero threatens corporal punishment for Caliban's curses, Caliban remarks in an aside

> I must obey, his Art is of such pow'r
> It would controll my Dams god Setebos,
> And make a vassaile of him.

At the start of Act II, scene 2, Caliban again curses Prospero, adding uneasily, "his Spirits heare me, / And yet I needes must curse." Caliban, who inherited the island from his mother Sycorax before Prospero was shipwrecked there, feels (quite properly, for an aborigine or a psychic depth) that he has been unfairly deprived of his rights and powers. When Caliban, Stephano, and Trinculo plot the murder of Prospero, Caliban keeps warning them of the danger: "if he awake, / From toe to crowne hee'l fill our skins with pinches, / Make us strange stuffe." He begs the drunken louts to hurry: "we shall loose our time, / And all be turn'd to Barnacles, or to Apes / With foreheads villanous low." In Act V, when the plotters are brought in by Ariel to be punished, Caliban's desperate comment, before his speech of repentance, is "I shall be pincht to death."

As a type of the artist, Prospero often misleads, but unlike Iago he misleads in a good cause, toward the working out of his redemptive happy ending. Instructed by Prospero, Ariel in his appearance as a harpy tells Alonso that the powers have "bereft" him of a son, which Alonso understands as meaning that his son is dead; we in the audience know that "bereft" conceals a joke about removal from his father's house to marry, which the play develops when Prospero tells Alonso, in Act V, that he in turn has lost a daughter "In this last Tempest." Prospero misleads Ferdinand with his harshness and abuse, before confessing, in Act IV: "All thy vexations / Were but my trials of thy love." Prospero's magical calamities and misleading do no real harm. When Miranda expresses her distress, in Act I, scene 2, at the terrible shipwreck caused by Prospero's tempest, Prospero assures her: "Tell your pitteous heart / There's no harme done." We see the magical harmlessness of the tempest and shipwreck in graphic imagery in Act II, scene 1, when Gonzalo proclaims that the clothing of the shipwrecked men has been freshened and renewed by their experience. In Act V, Alonso and his court finally see Ferdinand and Miranda playing chess, not only is everyone alive and well, but the wrecked ship is then revealed to be as "tyte, and yare, and bravely rig'd, as when / We first put out to Sea." We get an elaborate metaphor for Prospero's sort of benign magic, his benevolent dictatorship, in Gonzalo's long speech in Act II, scene 1, describing the utopia (borrowed from Montaigne) that he would produce if he ruled the island.

Prospero is not only a type of the artist as benign magician, he is specifically a type of the playwright, effecting his magic by the creation of dramatic situations. He announces in the second scene of the first act that he will produce a play within the play, which we might call "The Trials of Ferdinand." Prospero says of the lovers:

> They are both in eythers pow'rs: But this swift busines
> I must uneasie make, least too light winning
> Make the prize light.

For the final discovery in Act V, Prospero produces another playlet, in which he discards his island garb and costumes himself as the once and future Duke:

> not one of them
> That yet lookes on me, or would know me: Ariell,
> Fetch me the Hat, and Rapier in my Cell,
> I will discase me, and my selfe present
> As I was sometime Millaine.

Prospero's apparition to Alonso and his court of Ferdinand and Miranda playing chess, which he calls to "bring forth a wonder," is another such dramatic staging, although here the metaphor for art is doubled, since the apparition of the lovers is a work of art, while the chess game itself (one of the few chess allusions in Shakespeare) is a work of art within the work of art (as it might be in Nabokov). The final tribute to Prospero's artistry as a dramatist is Alonso's comment in the last act: "This is as strange a Maze, as ere men trod."

Like Iago, Prospero speaks directly to the audience, but his addresses are of a very different order. His most famous one in the play, the great speech in Act IV, is not only an obvious metaphor for the stage performance (with its joke about the Globe Theatre)

but beyond that is a larger comment on the transience
of art and illusion, even of life itself. He says

> Our Revels now are ended: These our actors,
> (As I foretold you) were all Spirits, and
> Are melted into Ayre, into thin Ayre,
> And like the baselesse fabricke of this vision
> The Clowd-capt Towres, the gorgeous Pallaces,
> The solemne Temples, the great Globe it selfe,
> Yea, all which it inherit, shall dissolve,
> And like this insubstantiall Pageant faded
> Leave not a racke behinde: we are such stuffe
> As dreames are made on; and our little life
> Is rounded with a sleepe.

Prospero makes a comparable speech about the illusion of art in Act V, announcing:

> The charme dissolves apace,
> And as the morning steales upon the night
> (Melting the darknesse) so their rising sences
> Begin to chace the ignorant fumes that mantle
> Their cleerer reason.

Prospero's epilogue is still a third such, but the flat-
ness of the verse and the weakness of the language
lead me, in the company of many Shakespeare scholars, to reject it as spurious.

Prospero is not only poet and playwright, he is
stage illusionist and director. In Act III, scene 3, he
appears invisible at the top of the scene, to "Solemne
and strange Musicke," as his spirits bring in the ban-

quet to Alonso and his court. This is the music or harmony theme, and it is shortly followed by a compen-
sating illusion of the tempest or discord theme, as
Ariel dressed as a harpy enters to "Thunder and
Lightning" to make the banquet vanish before it can
be eaten, and lecture the villains on the extent of their
wickedness. In the next act, Prospero instructs Ariel
to arrange another illusion, the masque, for Ferdinand
and Miranda, explaining somewhat lamely,

> for I must
> Bestow upon the eyes of this yong couple
> Some vanity of mine Art: it is my promise,
> And they expect it from me.

During a pause in the masque, Ferdinand compli-
ments Prospero on it: "This is a most majesticke vision, and / Harmonious charmingly." ("Charmingly"
perhaps means, as Staunton says, not "delightfully"
but "magically.") Prospero's reply explaining the vision is one of the play's key metaphors for the artist:

> Spirits, which by mine Art
> I have from their confines call'd to enact
> My present fancies.

As the masque is about to resume, he calls on Ferdinand and Miranda for silence, and explains the fragile
nature of illusion: "hush, and be mute / Or else our
spell is mar'd." Perhaps the play's most delightful
comment of all on the nature of artistic illusion comes

86

in Act V, when Prospero tells the amazed Gonzalo "You doe yet taste / Some subtleties o'th'Isle." Steevens explains this in a learned and instructive note, revealing the metaphor to be drawn from another illusionary art. He writes:

> A phrase adopted from ancient cookery and confectionery. When a dish was so contrived as to appear unlike what it really was, they called it a *subtilty*. Dragons, castles, trees, etc. made out of sugar had the like denomination. Froissart complains much of this practice, which often led him into mistakes at dinner.

The dual purpose of Prospero's artistic illusions is the ancient dual purpose of art, to please but ultimately to instruct. In Act I, scene 2, he calls himself Miranda's "Schoolemaster," and this is one of his roles in the play. On his arrival on the island, he taught Caliban such things as the names of the sun and the moon, for which Caliban had never before had any names (the artist is a kind of Adam, freshly naming the things of Creation). He or Miranda (the speaker is a matter of scholarly debate) taught Caliban language itself, and, in a famous remark, Caliban offers ironic thanks to either or both of them: "You taught me Language, and my profit on't / Is, I know how to curse." As he is a schoolmaster, Prospero is also a director of illusion. He presents the first sight of Ferdinand, the only man she has ever seen other than her father, to Miranda in terms of directing a scene:

The fringed Curtaines of thine eye advance,
And say what thou see'st yond.

When Ferdinand and Miranda leave the stage at the
end of the first scene of the third act, we discover that
their whole encounter and prompt falling in love has
been directed by Prospero. He remarks: "So glad of
this as they I cannot be, / Who are surpriz'd with
all."

As the purpose of Iago's art is consistently malign,
so the purpose of Prospero's art, with all its magic,
misleading, dramatization, and illusion creating, is
benign. It is devoted to the betterment of men and the
righting of wrong, the traditional poetic themes of
love and justice. In Act III, scene 3, Prospero
describes Sebastian and Anthonio as "worse then
divels"; by Act V they are chastened, restrained, and
perhaps even repentant devils (Alonso rights the
wrong they collectively committed, and begs Prospero's pardon for their misdeeds). This island of art is
a place of magical transformation, and its key image
of transformation is the "Sea-change," the transmuta-
tion into the precious and imperishable, of Ariel's
song:

> Full fadom five thy Father lies,
> Of his bones are Corrall made:
> Those are pearles that were his eyes,
> Nothing of him that doth fade,
> But doth suffer a Sea-change
> Into something rich, and strange:

The full sea change produced by Prospero's island is summed up by Gonzalo in Act V:

> O rejoyce
> Beyond a common joy, and set it downe
> With gold on lasting Pillers: In one voyage
> Did Claribell her husband finde at Tunis,
> And Ferdinand her brother, found a wife,
> Where he himselfe was lost: Prospero, his Dukedome
> In a poore Isle: and all of us, our selves,
> When no man was his owne.

Even Caliban is transformed and repentant, and for reward he recovers his island at the end. As Prospero sends him to Prospero's cell and adds "as you looke / To have my pardon, trim it handsomely," Caliban repudiates his false gods and has an intimation of true value:

> Aye that I will: and Ile be wise hereafter,
> And seeke for grace: what a thrice double Asse
> Was I to take this drunkard for a god?
> And worship this dull foole?

In the course of his reformations, Prospero punishes before he forgives. In Act IV, Stephano and Trinculo, the drunken clowns, are led through endless briars and thorns before they are deposited up to their chins in a "filthy mantled poole," and Prospero threatens further, of them and Caliban, "I will plague them all, / Even to roaring." In a dialogue with Ariel early in

Act V, Prospero shows his ultimate intention in regard to Alonso and his entire court:

Ariel.　　　　. . . your charm so strongly works'em
　　　　　　That if you now beheld them, your
　　　　　　affections
　　　　　　Would become tender.
Prospero. Does thou thinke so, Spirit?
Ariel.　　Mine would, Sir, were I humane.
Prospero. And mine shall.

Explaining that "the rarer Action is / In vertue, then in vengeance," he then instructs Ariel:

　　Goe, release them Ariell,
　My Charmes Ile breake, their sences Ile restore,
　And they shall be themselves.

Eventually Prospero somewhat grudgingly forgives even his wicked usurping and murderous brother Anthonio: "I do forgive / Thy rankest fault." *

In the play's key metaphor for the sea change (first fully worked out by G. Wilson Knight, who found it to be the over-all metaphor for the whole of Shake-

---

* We should note that many other characters in the play are lesser types of the artist, spokes radiating out from Prospero's hub. Thus Ariel is the performing artist who plays the score that Prospero has composed, or enacts the drama that he has written; Caliban sets up as a rival composer and playwright but lacks the powers to bring off his work of art; Gonzalo, in his long utopian speech imagining himself as the ruler of a similar magical island, is an imaginary or surrogate artist; Anthonio is a malign dramatist on the order of Iago, but, like Caliban in this benign magical setting, an impotent one; and so forth.

speare's work), Prospero turns tempest into music, discord into harmony (as Iago turns harmony into discord). The play opens with the discord of the tempest itself, "A tempestuous noise of Thunder and Lightning heard." Other examples of discord, mainly in the clownish subplot, are: Stephano's drunken singing "a very scurvy tune" in Act II, scene 2; Caliban's drunken singing in the same scene; Stephano and Trinculo's drunken singing which gets Ariel's tune wrong in Act III, scene 2; the thunder and lightning with which Ariel enters disguised; the conspiracy of Caliban with the drunken clowns to murder Prospero, which suddenly turns the harmony of the masque "to a strange hollow and confused noise" during which the masquers vanish. The spirit dogs that hound the three conspirators are a discord, as is the conspirators' reaction, described by Ariel as "Harke, they rore"; the play's final discord is the terrible noise which awakens Botolph and the sailors:

> strange, and severall noises
> Of roring, shreeking, howling, gingling chaines,
> And mo diversities of sounds, all horrible.

Harmonious music is the characteristic sound of Prospero's enchanted island, and in the course of the action all the tempest and discord are transmuted into it. In Act III, scene 2, Caliban gives an eloquent and lovely description of the music of this magical island of art. He says, to reassure Stephano and Trinculo:

Be not affeard, the Isle is full of noises,
Sounds, and sweet aires, that give delight and hurt
    not:
Sometimes a thousand twangling Instruments
Will hum about mine eares; and sometime voices,
That if I then had wak'd after long sleepe,
Will make me sleepe againe, and then in dreaming,
The clouds methought would open, and shew riches
Ready to drop upon me, that when I wak'd
I cri'de to dreame againe.

Stephano's comment is typical of the delusion which Yeats calls "the chief temptation of the artist, creation without toil." Stephano says:

This will prove a brave kingdome to me,
Where I shall have my Musicke for nothing.

Earlier, in Act II, scene 1, Ariel had appeared invisibly to Alonso and his court, playing "solemne Musicke"; now, in Act III, scene 3, Prospero appears to them invisibly, accompanied by "Solemne and strange Musicke," along with the spirits bringing in the banquet. Alonso asks "What harmony is this? my good friends, harke," and Gonzalo answers "Marvellous sweet Musicke." In the fourth act, when Prospero warns Ferdinand against deflowering Miranda before their wedding, he does so in a musical metaphor: the "sweet aspersion" that would otherwise fall from the heavens on their marriage bed will turn into "discord." The masque then demonstrates these harmonies when

92

the goddesses break into song, and the lovers hear "Juno sings her blessings on you." The final judgment and reconciliation in the fifth act are preceded by Ariel's entering again with "Solemne musicke," and Prospero comments, "A solemne Ayre, and the best comforter, / To an unsetled fancie." Music is clearly therapeutic, even somewhat redemptive; thus Mrs. Jameson in her *Characteristics of Women* charmingly explains Miranda's sweetness with the statement: "The very air, made vocal by her father's art, floated in music around her."

Finally, then, Prospero is the figure of the artist at his most glorified (as Iago is at his most debased), with the artist's paradoxical combination of great magical powers and great unworldliness. Miranda begins the play's second scene by asking (somewhat rhetorically) whether Prospero has raised the tempest "by your Art"; shortly afterward Prospero asks her to help him off with his "Magick garment," which he addresses on the ground: "Lye there my Art"; he then assures her that all is safely under his control, saying:

> The direfull spectacle of the wracke which
>   touch'd
> The very vertue of compassion in thee:
> I have with such provision in mine Art
> So safely ordered, that there is no soule
> No not so much perdition as an hayre
> Betid to any creature in the vessell

Then Prospero tells Miranda of his past history as Duke of Milan, explaining that "the liberall Artes" entirely occupied him, "those being all my studie," and that he abandoned worldly power in the state to his brother Anthonio, "transported / And rapt in secret studies"; "I thus neglecting worldly ends," his brother betrayed him and supplanted him in his dukedom. In Anthonio's opinion, Prospero's "Librarie / Was Dukedome large enough" for him, but the implication is clear that Prospero, without making any conscious choice, was more or less of the same opinion. When Prospero was banished, Gonzalo furnished the boat with books from Prospero's library, "volumes, that / I prize above my Dukedome."

The paradox here, and it is a major theme of the play, is that Prospero's unworldly bookish art is ultimately more powerful than any worldly power, and it enables him to overcome and redeem the villains and restore the order of justice. In the same scene, Prospero tells Miranda that "bountifull Fortune" has brought his enemies into his power, but he has collaborated in it by raising the tempest, and says almost boastfully that he knows "by my prescience" that this is his destined moment to restore his worldly fortunes. Prospero continues with the same moderate boastfulness, or pride of achievement in his bookish learning, in later remarks.

The final statement of the extent of his magical powers comes in the famous speech in Act V concluding with his abdication of them (which commentators, since the poet Thomas Campbell in 1838, have generally read as Shakespeare's own symbolic renunciation of his literary career). He says:

                    I have bedymn'd
The Noone-tide Sun, call'd forth the mutenous windes,
And twixt the greene Sea, and the azur'd vault
Set roaring warre: To the dread ratling Thunder
Have I given fire, and rifted Joves stowt Oke
With his owne Bolt: The strong bass'd promontorie
Have I made shake, and by the spurs pluckt up
The Pyne, and Cedar. Graves at my command
Have wak'd their sleepers, op'd, and let 'em forth
By my so potent Art. But this rough Magicke
I here abjure: and when I have requir'd
Some heavenly Musicke (which even now I do)
To worke mine end upon their Sences, that
This Ayrie-charme is for, I'le breake my staffe,
Bury it certaine fadomes in the earth,
And deeper then did ever Plummet sound
Ile drowne my booke.

(The contrast here with Iago's "From this time forth,
I never will speake word" is wonderfully suggestive.)

It has been much easier, for obvious reasons, for
scholars and critics (including some loonies) to see
Prospero as a type of the artist than for them to see
Iago similarly. As Furnivall wrote in 1877, "The general consent of critics and readers identifies Shakespeare, in the ripeness of his art and power, more with
Prospero than with any other of his characters." Coleridge was one of the first to make the identification,
observing almost casually, "Prospero (the very
Shakespeare himself, as it were, of the tempest)."

95

Campbell wrote (with a certain confusion of Prospero's staff and book):

> Shakespeare, as if conscious that it would be his last, and as if inspired to typify himself, has made its hero a natural, a dignified, and benevolent magician, who could conjure up spirits from the vasty deep, and command supernatural agency by the most seemingly natural and simple means. . . . Here Shakespeare himself is Prospero, or rather the superior genius who commands both Prospero and Ariel. But the time was approaching when the potent sorcerer was to break his staff, and to bury it fathoms in the ocean—'deeper than did ever plummet sound.' That staff has never been, and never will be, recovered.

Émile Montégut wrote in 1865, in the *Revue des Deux Mondes:*

> *The Tempest* is clearly the last of Shakespeare's dramas, and, under the form of an allegory, is the dramatic last will and testament of the great poet, . . . in a word, this drama is a poetic synthesis, or, as Prospero would express it in the language of a magician, it is a *microcosm* of that dramatic world which his imagination had created.

This is unexceptional enough, but Montégut then goes on to make it a microcosm of the history of the

English theatre, to make Caliban a portrait of "—let us boldly call him Marlowe,—a devilish creature with a criminal imagination, a soul of the damned, whom education debased instead of refining, and whose savagery seemed merely to increase under all the resources of civilization." Similarly Sebastian and Anthonio are "some George Chapman, or some John Marston, egged on by jealousy and hate, perhaps, also by the instigations of that dog of a Ben Jonson."

James Russell Lowell wrote in *Among My Books* in 1870: "For in Prospero shall we not recognize the Artist himself, . . . who has forfeited a shining place in the world's eye by devotion to his art, and who, turned adrift on the ocean of life on the leaky carcass of a boat, has shipwrecked on the Fortunate Island (as men always do who find their true vocation) where he is absolute lord." By Lowell's time this was all conventional enough, certainly, but Lowell added a Coleridgean specificity: "But consider for a moment if ever the Imagination has been so embodied as in Prospero, the Fancy as in Ariel." Dowden, in *Shakspere—His Mind and Art* in 1875, wrote a similar interpretation of Prospero as "the man of genius, the great artist," adding two specific equations: "He bears with him Art in its infancy—the marvelous child, Miranda," and, closer on the scale of looniness to Montégut:

And who is Ferdinand? Is he not, with his gallantry and his beauty, the young Fletcher in conjunction with whom Shakspere worked upon *The Two Noble Kinsmen* and *Henry VIII?*

(Dowden at least had the grace to apologize for all this as a playful and innocent, "if trifling attempt to read the supposed allegory.")

Furnivall wrote in 1877: "The poet uses his magic to wield the fairy world and the powers of nature for the highest possible end—the winning back to good, of human souls given over to evil." Sir Edward Strachey in 1890 produced essentially the same reading, but made it clearer that this was a literary rather than a clerical function: "a tempest raised by Art, to work moral ends with actual men and women, and then to sink into a calm. And in such a storm or calm we have the very idea of a Play or Drama." Also in 1890, Dr. Garnett put the case most moderately:

> That this Quixotic height of magnanimity should not surprise, that it should seem quite in keeping with the character, proves how deeply this character has been drawn from Shakespeare's own nature. Prospero is not Shakespeare, but the play is in a certain measure autobiographical . . . It is interesting to compare Prospero with the Faust of *The Second Part;* who, far more distinctly than Shakespeare's creation, impersonates the author and sums up his final view of life.

G. Wilson Knight, in *Myth and Miracle* (1929), refers to "the magic island of great poetry" in the play;

and Northrop Frye, in his introduction to an edition of *The Tempest* in 1959, calls Prospero "a creative artist."

At the other extreme are interpretations which see Prospero as so much the creative artist that they end by making him God the Creator. Edward R. Russell in the *Theological Review* in 1876 presented a full-scale reading of Prospero as a portrait of "Omnipotence" in "his grave struggle with powers of evil." There is space here only to quote its conclusion:

> . . . . this most gracious creation of Shakespeare's tenderest mood of wistful theological thought. That his thought was theological we cannot doubt, ethereal and sparkling as was its expression. It is unlikely that the scheme of *The Tempest* could have had any other origin than the contemplations to which we attribute it; and it is impossible that such analogies to the Divine government should have gone unnoticed under his eye as they passed in the act of creation from his pen.

Myth and Miracle also calls Prospero "the 'God' of the *Tempest* universe," and C.J. Sisson in "The Magic of Prospero" in *Shakespeare Survey* in 1958 deals with him variously as "God or Providence" or "the Vicar of God."

Then there are the Freudian critics, who have chosen to see Iago as a neurotic but Prospero as an artist. Freud read *The Tempest* as autobiographical

99

but, to his shame, as autobiographical of the Earl of Oxford. Hanns Sachs, in *Imago* in 1919, interpreted Prospero as Shakespeare, the island as poetry ("noises that hurt not") and Miranda as art, but then either fell into Montégut's nonsense or copied him: Caliban represents the rough style of the older Tudor dramatists; the clowns are Shakespeare's imitators, Ferdinand is Fletcher, and so forth. Finally, Norman N. Holland has produced something closer to an orthodox psychoanalytic interpretation than either Freud or Sachs did: "Prospero deals with these Oedipal and aggressive impulses very much as a writer-director of plays might, by putting them into dramatic characters and moving them through a plot toward catharsis." This seems essentially to read the play as a tragedy, rather than the comedy culminating in "the magic wedding of the world" (to use a term borrowed from my friend and colleague, Catherine Osgood Foster) that it is. Holland's formulation, in my view, would better fit Iago's role as playwright in *Othello*, building up pity and terror to a final tragic catharsis.

[4]

THIS APPROACH is psychoanalytic criticism, and its Iago is motivated by strong latent homosexuality (or acts as does a person so motivated). This is not only abundantly clear in the play, but it is clearly of Shakespeare's deliberate contrivance, since there is no trace of any such thing in the story he got from his source, Giovanbattista Giraldi Cinthio's *Hecatommithi*, and all the evidences of it in the play are Shakespeare's alterations and additions. In Cinthio's tale, the Ensign falls passionately in love with Disdemona, and he really does believe that she loves the Cassio character; he is, in short, motivated by normal heterosexual jealousy. Iago neither loves Desdemona nor believes for a moment that she loves Cassio, despite several statements he makes to the contrary. It is he who unconsciously loves both Othello and Cassio; that love is repressed and, by the defense mechanism called "reaction formation," turned into hate.

In the first scene of the first act, Iago expresses his hostility to Cassio, as knowing nothing more of battles "then a Spinster" and as "almost damn'd in a faire Wife," curious terms for a handsome and virile bachelor; and he twice strongly denies any affection for Othello in speeches already quoted, "not I for love" in the heart-on-the-sleeve speech, and again in the speech punning on "sign." Another ingredient of Iago's strong latent homosexuality is his contempt for women and his disgust with heterosexual love and marriage, both themes pervading the play. The line about Cassio, "almost damn'd in a faire Wife," is quite interesting in this connection. Whether it means, as the Cowden-Clarkes understood it, "A fellow who would almost go to perdition for a handsome woman," or, as J. J. B. Workard explained it, " 'fellow' of so soft a character that a similar disposition would be 'almost damned in a fair wife,' " the views of women are equally scornful, and if it means what Steevens thought (and Malone concurred in), "he is not yet *completely damned*, because he is not *absolutely married*," the view of marriage is no more lovely. The scene also contains a number of clear evidences of Iago's disgust with heterosexuality itself, which he tends to put in bestial imagery, as he does throughout the play (expressing what Heilman calls Iago's "barn-yard view of life"). Iago cries up to Brabantio, "an old blacke Ram / Is tupping your white Ewe," then continues

> . . . you'le have your Daughter cover'd with a Barbary horse, you'le have your Nephewes neigh to you, you'le have Coursers for Cozens: and Gennets for Germaines.

His final remark along these lines is the most gross,

"your Daughter and the Moore, are making the Beast with two backs."

In the second scene, telling Cassio the news about Othello, Iago changes his metaphor, informing him "he to night hath boarded a Land Carract," which Staunton explains as a large ship like a Spanish galleon, adding, "the compound in the text appears to have been a dissolute expression."

In the third scene, alone with Rodorigo, Iago combines the two sorts of imagery. He proclaims: "Ere I would say, I would drowne my selfe for the love of a Ginney Hen, I would change my Humanity with a Baboone," and Steevens explains "guinea hen" as "Anciently the cant term for a prostitute." Iago continues with an assurance to Rodorigo of the sort that he uses regularly to dupe him, but here in a psychoanalytic perspective we have to see a powerful unconscious wish underlying the duping. "It cannot be long that Desdemona should continue her love to the Moore," he says, "nor he his to her. . . . These Moores are changeable in their wils." Iago goes on to state his own emotional investment in the matter (more than he realizes). He says, "I have told thee often, and I re-tell thee againe, and againe, I hate the Moore. . . . If thou canst Cuckold him, thou dost thy selfe a pleasure, me a sport." After Rodorigo has been sent off, Iago has his soliloquy to conclude the act, and tells the audience:

> I hate the Moore,
> And it is thought abroad, that 'twixt my sheets
> He ha's done my Office.

(Heilman comments excellently on the inadequacy of that "and" in place of the expected "since.") This charge, which is patently untrue, is flatly contradicted by other things that Iago says of Othello, and after one more repetition in Act II, scene 1, is entirely forgotten. Such unconvincing explanations, dismissed by other approaches as either Coleridge's "motive-hunting" or as the same sort of lying to the audience as Iago's lying to Rodorigo, have great significance in a psychoanalytic perspective. They reflect the unconscious wish that Othello go to bed with him, disguised by projection as the possibility that Othello has gone to bed with Æmilia,* and further defended against by being made rumor rather than his own idea. More deeply, they show the characteristic "castration anxiety" or "negative Oedipus complex," which is one of the possible reactions to the Oedipal ambivalence toward the father, in which the active or strongly latent homosexual identifies with his mother or a mother-surrogate and in fantasy enjoys his father sexually. Othello takes Iago's place with his wife as the more virile and dominant figure; in another aspect, it is the common latent homosexual fantasy, obsessive in the work of Joyce, of two men symbolically uniting sexu-

* The First Folio misprint of the line as "She ha's done my Office." should serve as a useful reminder that *everyone*, even a typesetter, is a latent homosexual in the Freudian system.

ally by sharing the body of the same woman.

In the first scene of the second act, Iago, in his banter with Desdemona, makes a comic speech mocking the inappropriateness of women's acts to their settings; that is, he defines the unnaturalness of women by means of the inappropriateness of their scene-act ratios. Iago says:

> Come on, come on: you are Pictures out of doore: Bells in your Parlours: Wilde-Cats in your Kitchens: Saints in your Injuries: Divels being offended: Players in your Huswiferie, and Huswives in your Beds.

Desdemona then encourages him to improvise in rhymed couplets on the subject of women, and several of his improvisations have his characteristic nasty note of contempt for women. Iago recites:

There's none so foule and foolish thereunto,
But do's foule pranks, which faire, and wise-ones do.

He continues, along more indecent lines:

> She that in wisedome never was so fraile,
> To change the Cods-head for the Salmons taile.

Later in the scene, when Iago is alone with Rodorigo, he expresses similar statements about the natural infidelity of women, in assuring him that Desdemona will soon become tired of Othello, if she is not so already. He says, in prose:

When the Blood is made dull with the Act of
Sport, there should be a game to enflame it, and
to give Satiety a fresh appetite.

Iago adds that Desdemona has already developed a
passion for Cassio, adducing as evidence "Didst thou
not see her paddle with the palme of his hand?" When
Rodorigo objects that this was merely courtesy, Iago
continues his characteristic argument about the wickedness of women. "Leacherie by this hand: an Index,
and obscure prologue to the History of Lust and foule
Thoughts," he says. After Rodorigo is dismissed, Iago
treats the audience to a soliloquy in which he makes
the unconvincing claim that he too lusts after Desdemona, in a fashion, and repeats (for the last time in
the play) his suspicion of Othello. He announces:

> Now I do love her too,
> Not out of absolute Lust, (though peradventure
> I stand accomptant for as great a sin)
> But partely led to dyet my Revenge,
> For that I do suspect the lustie Moore
> Hath leap'd into my Seate.

The complex dynamics of projection and other defense mechanisms in the jealousy has been analyzed
above, but here we can note additionally that the desire he expresses for Desdemona is the simplest sort of
displacement of his desire for Othello. Iago then announces his intentions of revenge:

> And nothing can, or shall content my Soule
> Till I am eeven'd with him, wife, for wife.

Or fayling so, yet that I put the Moore,
At least into a Jelouzie so strong
That judgement cannot cure.

What is interesting here is that even as he announces
his intention of cuckolding Othello, Iago gives up the
idea, and replaces it with the real plan which he actually puts into effect, to madden him with jealousy.
This has a perfect psychoanalytic rightness, since the
emotion Iago actually does seem to feel (in this perspective) is intense jealousy of Desdemona, for being
to Othello what he would like to be. He goes on, as the
soliloquy approaches its end, to add his other and
equally unconvincing suspicion, "(For I feare Cassio
with my Night-Cape too)." In this doubling of the
suspicion, we can see the full extent of his defense mechanisms. Iago disguises his homosexual impulses by
projecting them onto Othello and Cassio (that is, onto
any virile men who attract him), and further disguises them as heterosexual, so that Othello and Cassio either lust after or have enjoyed his wife. (The
sequence is from "I want them" to "They want me" to
"They want my wife.") As the speech's final nasty
irony, the result of this vicious betrayal of three people will be to "Make the Moore thanke me, love me,
and reward me."

In the second scene in the act, after Cassio has been
disgraced, Othello's terminology develops this ironic
theme, when he asks Iago to tell him who began the
quarrel, with "On thy love I charge thee." Iago's answer, in an interesting unconscious homosexual im-

agery, is that until the quarrel broke out, Montano and Cassio had been "like Bride, and Groome / Devesting them for Bed." In assuring the discharged Cassio that he should plead his case to Desdemona, Iago explains contemptuously, "Our General's Wife, is now the Generall," which in a psychoanalytic perspective again reveals the reversal of sexual role and identity which is the heart of Iago's motivation. In his following soliloquy to the audience, proclaiming Desdemona's power over Othello, Iago adds "Even as her Appetite shall play the God, / With his weake Function," revealing not only his familiar view of women as lust-mad, but flatly contradicting his statement in the scene before about "the lustie Moore," so that in a sense each exposes the other, and we can see that he is prepared to state any view of Othello's potency which will fit his rationalization of the moment. Iago goes on to explain that as Cassio pleads his case with Desdemona and can thus be presented as implicating them both, Iago will work on Othello:

> Ile powre this pestilence into his eare:
> That she repeales him, for her bodies Lust.

The image of pouring anything into the ear (even pestilence) is, as *Antony and Cleopatra* makes abundantly clear, a strongly sexual, here homosexual, one; a traditional displacement upward of the genital or anal.

In Act III, scene 3, as Iago begins his terrible seduction of Othello, Othello recurs to an earlier ironic motif in begging to be seduced. He says, "If thou do'st

Hamlet?

108

love me, / Shew me thy thought." In a nasty genital pun, Iago says of Desdemona, "I know our Country disposition well," and continues it shortly afterward in "her Country formes." After he has poured a considerable amount of pestilence into Othello's ear, Iago makes his habitual reticent apology:

> But I am much too blame:
> I humbly do beseech you of your pardon
> For too much loving you.

This is entirely true, in a sense of which neither is conscious, but in the world of consciousness it is more lying and hypocrisy, and Iago's reward for it is Othello's immediate answer, "I am bound to thee for ever." Iago goes on, in another unconscious projection, to speak of Desdemona's "Thoughts unnaturall." Later in the scene, when Iago and Æmilia are alone together, and she brings him the all-important handkerchief, she announces it as "I have a thing for you," and Iago responds automatically with another of his slurs on the female genitals, "It is a common thing." When Othello returns, desperately upset and made somewhat warier by his interview with Desdemona and his thoughts about her, Iago warms to his seduction, and his imagery for heterosexual sex returns to its earlier coarseness. When Othello asks for some evidence that would satisfy him, Iago says

> Would you the super-vision grossely gape on?
> Behold her top'd?

He continues, reverting to his habitual bestial imagery,

> It is impossible you should see this,
> Were they as prime as Goates, as hot as
>   Monkeyes,
> As salt as Wolves in pride.

When Othello continues to ask for concrete evidence
of Desdemona's infidelity, Iago produces the imaginative masterpiece of all his scheming in the play, his
improvisation of "Cassio's dream." He says:

> I lay with Cassio lately,
> And being troubled with a raging tooth,
> I could not sleepe. There are a kinde of men,
> So loose of Soule, that in their sleepes will mutter
> Their Affayres: one of this kinde is Cassio:
> In sleepe I heard him say, sweet Desdemona,
> Let us be wary, let us hide our Loves,
> And then (Sir) would he gripe, and wring my
>   hand:
> Cry, oh sweet Creature: then kisse me hard,
> As if he pluckt up kisses by the rootes,
> That grew upon my lippes, laid his Leg ore my
>   Thigh,
> And sigh, and kisse, and then cry cursed Fate,
> That gave thee to the Moore.

The homosexual dynamics here are as simple and
clear as they are fascinating: Iago has turned himself
into a Desdemona for Cassio's sexual enjoyment on

the surface of the spurious dream, and for Othello's in the latent content. Note also how the eroticism begins with what Iago has observed, the holding of hands, and progresses logically from there to passionate kissing and then to straddling. Edwin Booth's note for playing the lines about gripping and wringing Iago's hand is: "Holds Othello's hand, which Othello draws with disgust from his grasp." Iago then adds his clincher: getting Othello to admit that "a Handkerchiefe / Spotted with Strawberries" was his first gift to Desdemona, he announces:

> I know not that: but such a Handkerchiefe
> (I am sure it was your wives) did I to day
> See Cassio wipe his Beard with.

The magical handkerchief has not only been given to Cassio, in Iago's imputation, but Cassio profanes it; as, when Othello is allowed to see Cassio appear to offer it to Bianca, he seems further to profane it. By this time Othello is thoroughly convinced, and soon afterwards seduced and seducer kneel together and swear loyalty to hatred and vengeance on Desdemona. Where this was a demonic pact in a theological perspective, in a psychoanalytic perspective it is a monstrous marriage vow, and it and Cassio's spurious dream are perhaps the two most blatant evidences of Iago's unconscious homosexual motivation. It is a most powerful scene. As he kneels beside Othello, Iago calls on

> You Elements, that clip us round about,
> Witnesse that heere Iago doth give up
> The execution of his wit, hands, heart,
> To wrong'd Othello's Service. Let him command,
> And to obey shall be in me remorse,
> What bloody businesse ever.

("Clip" means "embrace.") Othello promptly replies:

> I greet thy love
> Not with vaine thanks, but with acceptance
>   bounteous,
> And will upon the instant put thee too't.

Booth played the end of this scene with Iago quickly kneeling and kissing Othello's hand (from which there was no withdrawal in disgust). By this time, as Heilman brilliantly points out, Iago's "honesty" is not too far from what the term earlier meant in regard to Desdemona, the "chastity" or fidelity of a beloved.

In the fourth scene of the act, the dance of erotic hand symbolism continues. Othello takes Desdemona's hand, and comments that it is "Hot, hot, and moist." This is clearly displacement upward from her genitals, in Freudian terms; these terms are simply our way of saying what the Renaissance expressed as symbolization (as in the statement in *Antony and Cleopatra* that an oily palm is a fruitful prognostication). We get a second genital displacement a moment later, when Othello tells Desdemona the importance of the magical handkerchief, formerly his mother's, which he gave to Desdemona. The "Ægyptian" who had given it to his mother had assured her that it would serve as a charm to keep her husband's love as long as she had it,

> But if she lost it,
> Or made a Guift of it, my Fathers eye
> Should hold her loathed.

In the first scene of the fourth act, Iago continues his relentless pressure, conjuring up for Othello the image of Desdemona and Cassio naked together. Iago then returns to the displacement that is to become obsessive with Othello, and asks "But if I give my wife a Handkerchiefe," and when Othello asks "What then?" Iago answers smoothly,

> Why then 'tis hers (my Lord) and being hers,
> She may (I thinke) bestow't on any man.

Othello immediately rises to the bait and makes the equation: "She is Protectresse of her honor too." After Othello recovers from his trance, and complains about his state as a cuckold, Iago gives him more gross imagery, one of his characteristic non-reassuring reassurances, that the world is full of oblivious cuckolds, and that Othello is better off knowing than those whose fate it is "To lip a wanton in a secure Cowch; / And to suppose her chast." His next line, "And knowing what I am, I know what she shallbe," the revelation of Satanism in an earlier context, in a psychoanalytic perspective is a heavily ironic foreshadowing of her doom as a result of his unconsciously homosexual implacable hate. Iago then sets up Othello's spying on his interview with Cassio, promising him that he can watch Cassio's jeering expression as Iago gets him to recount the juicy details of

> Where, how, how oft, how long ago, and when
> He hath, and is againe to cope your wife.

In the conversation with Cassio, Iago gets the proper jeer by telling him, of the courtesan Bianca,

> She gives it out, that you shall marry her.
> Do you intend it?

Cassio's answer is "Ha, ha, ha." This scene is the final confirmation for Othello, and as he alternates plaints about the charms and gentleness of Desdemona with horrible threats to murder her, Iago adds, "Oh 'tis foule in her," and then gives his revolting advice about the killing:

> Do it not with poyson, strangle her in her bed,
> Even the bed she hath contaminated.

This speech was discussed earlier as an example of melodramatic villainy, but in this context it is a strikingly homosexual wish, the transformation of the heterosexual act into murder. Othello then concludes his ravings with "Goates, and Monkeys," picking up bestial imagery for Desdemona's sexuality which Iago had introduced in Act III.

By the second scene of the fourth act, Othello has been so far corrupted by Iago's view of the repulsive sexuality of women that he widens it to include Æmilia, whom he describes in a soliloquy after their conversation, when he has sent her off to fetch Desdemona, as "This is a subtile Whore: / A Closset Locke and Key of Villanous Secrets." When Desdemona appears, he announces that his choice is to discard their love,

> Or keepe it as a Cesterne, for foule Toades
> To knot and gender in.

In a theological context, this was an obvious Hellish image; in a psychoanalytic context it is even more clearly an image of sexual revulsion against his marriage, sprung from the seeds of imagery planted by Iago. Othello then questions Desdemona grossly, again along Iagoesque lines, "Are not you a Strumpet?" "What, not a Whore?" and comments sarcastically, in reaction to her serene assurance of virtue, "I tooke you for that cunning Whore of Venice, / That married with Othello" (the "cunning" even picking up Iago's genital pun).

The first scene of the fifth act is the revelation of Iago's unconscious homosexual love for Cassio too. He begins it in his opening soliloquy, as he waits impartially for Rodorigo to assassinate Cassio or be himself killed, when he says:

> If Cassio do remaine,
> He hath a dayly beauty in his life,
> That makes me ugly.

One can readily see the Satanic antagonism noted earlier, but in a psychoanalytic context we can see just as strongly the sexual attraction and envy. Othello then makes his brief entrance, decides that Iago has done his part of the joint task by killing Cassio, and goes off firm in the resolve to do his own share, announcing rhetorically, "Strumpet I come," and proclaiming madly, "Thy Bed lust-stain'd, shall with Lusts blood bee spotted." Iago then reenters, stabs the wounded Rodorigo to death, but is prevented from doing the same to the wounded Cassio by the appearance of Lodovico and Gratiano. He then becomes all loving attention. He binds up Cassio's wound with his (Iago's) shirt, borrows a garter from Gratiano for the bandage, and wishes for a sedan chair, "To beare him easily hence." This over-solicitude is of course put on to disguise his murderous hatred, but the irony is that it also gives expression to the unconscious homosexual love which in turn underlies that hatred. In the course of the scene, while all loving attention to Cassio, Iago insults Bianca when she appears as "O notable Strumpet" and "this Trash" (which, if they show the same hatred of women, at least have more factual justification than the similar terms for Desdemona); Iago's conclusion about Cassio's injury, expressed to Æmilia, is the flat "This is the fruits of whoring."

In the next and final scene of the play, when Othello enters Desdemona's bedroom to strangle her, he announces in soliloquy to the audience a kind of ultimate rationalization, "Yet she must dye, else shee'l betray more men," which not only picks up, in a most

116

melancholy and ironic fashion, the motif of the "Willow Song" she had earlier been singing (and he had not heard), but shows the extent to which Iago's sense of women as transcendentally wicked, beyond any given marriage, has taken charge of him. Soon after, begging for her life, Desdemona (again unconsciously) sums up the homosexual motivations that cause her death, when she tells Othello: "That death's unnaturall, that kils for loving," and continues, "Some bloody passion shakes your very Frame." Othello does not reply, except to revert to his usual "Out Strumpet" and "Downe Strumpet." He then smothers her, another example (as Kenneth Burke has shown) of psychoanalytic "displacement upward," shutting off an inoffensive orifice for the lower orifice which he regards as evil. After Æmilia enters, and Desdemona returns from death to proclaim her guiltlessness and Othello's innocence of the crime, Othello defends his deed to Æmilia in a series of less and less convincing (or convinced) charges: "She turn'd to folly, and she was a whore"; "Cassio did top her"; Iago, his informant, "hates the slime / That stickes on filthy deeds"; and, finally, almost convinced by Æmilia's passionate and ringing denials,

> 'Tis pittifull: but yet Iago knowes
> That she with Cassio, hath the Act of shame,
> A thousand times committed.

This last is in Iago's presence, and as Æmilia continues her exonerations of Desdemona and her charges against Iago, Iago gets to make the last two of his sexual charges, calling Æmilia "Villanous Whore" and saying, "Filth, thou lyest," before he stabs her and flees. The play's final word in this imagery of woman-hatred grown in the soil of unconscious homosexuality is Othello's, making amends for his earlier charge about the lecherous moistness (in displacement) of Desdemona's hand. Standing over her corpse, he proclaims in repentance and the return to true-seeing that comes at the end of the tragedy: "Cold, cold my Girle? / Even like thy Chastity." The rest is, psychoanalytically, silence.

The recognition that Iago speaks and behaves as if motivated by unconscious homosexual impulses came in our century, after Freud's discoveries. Before that, Iago's hostility to women had been almost universally noticed, but had rarely been seen as central to his motivation. One exception is the German, Johann Heinrich Voss, who, in 1806, in his introduction to his translation of the play, speaks of "the beginning of Act II, where Iago gives utterance to that hatred of the other sex which he subsequently puts into practice." Edwin Booth, as has been made abundantly clear above, played the role with a strong emphasis on Iago's sexual attraction to Othello, presumably on the basis of his dramaturgic intuition.

Since Freud, this recognition has been common to a number of his followers (although fewer than one might suppose).* It should be said that about nine-tenths of published psychoanalytic criticism of Shakespeare is worthless and infuriating, but the remaining tenth has useful things to say on the subject. Erich Wulffen analyzed the character of Iago as early as 1911 in *Shakespeares grosse Verbrecher*, but had little to say other than that Shakespeare failed to bring the character to life. Freud himself had mentioned the play in *The Interpretation of Dreams* in 1900, but only to note the handkerchief as an example of displacement. Dr. Daniel E. Schneider, in *The Psychoanalyst and the Artist* (1950), noted the additional significance that it was Othello's mother's handkerchief. W. H. Auden, in his essay on the play in *The Dyer's Hand* (1962) principally identified Iago as a kind of practical joker (a reading to rival Zachary Jackson's) but also defined him in psychoanalytic terms as a type of therapist, making unconscious conflicts conscious, although the type of therapist who kills instead of curing. A number of other Freudians have identified Shakespeare himself as a latent homosexual: Ernest Jones noted bisexual impulses in 1948 in the *International Journal of Psychoanalysis;* Harold Grier McCurdy in *The Personality of Shakespeare* (1953) found strong bisexual components in Shakespeare's nature; and Robert Boies Sharpe, in *Irony in the Drama* (1959), analyzed a basic homosexual com-

* I am grateful to Norman N. Holland's comprehensive and admirable survey of the literature, *Psychoanalysis and Shakespeare* (1966), for a good deal of the following information.

ponent in *Troilus and Cressida*.

The first directly homosexual psychoanalytic reading of Iago's motivation came in 1937, in Sir Laurence Olivier's flirtatious and "campy" performance of the role, which he had based on an interview with Jones, according to Marvin Rosenberg's *The Masks of Othello* (1961). Jones told Sir Laurence, according to Rosenberg, that "to his mind the clue to the play was not Iago's hatred for Othello, but his deep affection for him. His jealousy was not because he envied Othello's position, not because he was in love with Desdemona, but because he himself possessed a subconscious [*sic*] affection for the Moor, the homosexual foundation of which he did not understand."

The first psychoanalytic publication of such an interpretation of Iago's motivation was by Dr. Martin Wangh in "*Othello:* The Tragedy of Iago" in the *Psychoanalytic Quarterly* in 1950. He said essentially what Jones had said, but more strongly and going into considerable detail about Iago's impulses and defenses (he also threw in a wretched and useless interpretation of Cassio's non-dream, emphasizing Iago's aching tooth as a phallic symbol, and identified the handkerchief as a breast symbol). F. L. Lucas, in *Literature and Psychology* (1951) explains Iago's motivation as jealousy—he feels less loved than others such as Desdemona and Cassio—but Lucas adds that this idea is "too subtle for any audience." Gordon Ross Smith, in "Iago the Paranoiac" in *American Imago* (1959) extends Dr. Wangh's interpretation with further details, including Iago's repressed passion for

Cassio as well as Othello (while adding his own non-sense, the strawberries on the handkerchief as symbols for the *glans penis*). Robert Rogers in "Endopsychic Drama in *Othello*" in *Shakespeare Quarterly* (1969) extends this reading still further, treating Othello, Iago, and Cassio as three Freudian decompositions of one complete self. *

Not surprisingly, several psychoanalytic writers or writers influenced by psychoanalysis have denied the Satanic explanation by translating it into defense mechanisms of the ego. J. I. M. Stewart, in *Character and Motive in Shakespeare* (1949), remarks that the devil in the play, like all devils, represents a projection; and Rosenberg observes that Iago seems to be, though passionless, quite perfectly human (and thus not the devil of some critics' readings). Finally, on the basis of Freud's observation that male delusional jealousy is a radical defense against tender impulses toward another man, several Freudians have found an answering unconscious homosexuality in Othello, among them Dr. Enrique Racker, in an article published in *Revista de Psicoanálisis* as early as 1945, and Dr. A. Bronson Feldman in *American Imago* in 1952–53, among others. This is a subject, however, which need not concern us here, since the equally fascinating topic of Othello's own motivations, along with Shakespeare's, will be reserved for the Conclusion.

* This theory of "decomposition" was partially anticipated as early as 1944 in Leo Kirschbaum's "The Modern Othello" in *English Literary History*, II, and by J. P. Sullivan in "The Machiavel and the Moor" in *Essays in Criticism* (1960).

[5]

THIS LAST CHAPTER demonstrates a history of ideas approach, and its Iago is a Renaissance "Machiavel." He is motivated, not by Machiavelli's actual ideas, which Shakespeare may or may not have known, but by the Elizabethan image of the wicked Florentine, based on Gentillet's *Contre-Machiavel* of 1576, translated into English by Simon Patericke the next year. (*The Prince* itself was not translated into English until 1640.) The ideas of *The Prince* are revolutionary for their time, but it is the natural sort of revolution of developing political science, and it was put in markedly non-inflammatory terms. The ideas of *The Prince* would seem to have three principal strands, insofar as their implications go for a contemporary reader: a pragmatic "realism" which holds that the end justifies the means; a wholly secular or thisworldly set of criteria for success, which seem to ignore otherworldly sanctions; and a cynicism about human nature: man is naturally selfish, false, cowardly, and so forth.

The contrast between the ideas of the real Machiavelli and Gentillet's *Contre-Machiavel* is clear from

even the briefest quotation: Gentillet's Machiavelli is
the author of "Contempt of God, perfidy, sodomy, tyr-
anny, cruelty, pillage, foreign usury and other detest-
able vices." The Elizabethan image of the Machiavel,
if it was not quite so extreme as this, was quite lurid
enough. He was a Satanic figure (Patricke said flatly
that he was "sent from Sathan"), power-mad, of
boundless energy and egoism; he was ruthless and di-
abolically cruel; he despised and mocked all religious
or ethical values, and valued only material things,
particularly gold and his own advancement. That all
of this wickedness found its spokesman in Florence is,
I think, the point of the curious praise that Cassio addresses to the departing Iago in Act III, scene 1, of
our play: "I never knew / A Florentine more kinde,
and honest." This is curious because Iago is not a
Florentine but a Venetian, and scholars since Malone
have taken it to mean that Cassio, who *is* a Florentine,
finds Iago equal to the best of his countrymen. This
only makes sense, however, if it is a joke between
Shakespeare and the audience: "I never knew an unprincipled scoundrel and cutthroat more kind and
honest than he."

Iago emerges as an image of the Machiavel from
the play's first speech, in which Rodorigo reminds him
that he has "had my purse, / As if the strings were
thine." Iago is in fact the grossest sort of materialist,
which he confirms in a remark with profound implications later in the act, "I know my price." Later in the
first scene, Iago shows the corollary contempt for eth-

ical or spiritual values in his speech to Rodorigo on the two sorts of service. He says:

> You shall marke
> Many a dutious and knee-crooking knave;
> That (doting on his owne obsequious bondage)
> Weares out his time, much like his Masters
>   Asse,
> For naught but Provender, & when he's old
>   Casheer'd.
> Whip me such honest knaves. Others there are
> Who trym'd in Formes, and visages of Dutie,
> Keepe yet their hearts attending on them-
>   selves,
> And throwing but showes of Service on their
>   Lords
> Doe well thrive by them.
> And when they have lin'd their Coates
> Doe themselves Homage.
> These Fellowes have some soule,
> And such a one do I professe my selfe.

This cold cynicism and skepticism of all values beyond material self-interest develops into a series of debunking speeches later in the play: the first of these, on virtue, is in Act I, scene 3, when Iago tells Rodorigo, "Vertue? A figge, 'tis in our selves that we are thus, or thus."

The implications of Iago's "I know my price" have their great flowering in the third scene of the first act. Iago interrupts his advice to Rodorigo with no fewer

than ten variants of the same materialist injunction:
"Put Money in thy purse," "I say put Money in thy
purse," "Put Money in thy purse," "put but Money in
thy purse," "fill thy purse with Money," "Therefore,
put Money in thy purse," "Make all the Money thou
canst," "therefore make Money," "Go make Money,"
and "provide thy Money." Rodorigo, overwhelmed,
exits saying "Ile sell all my Land," and Iago reveals to
the audience that his advice was something less than
disinterested: "Thus do I ever make my Foole, my
purse."

In Act II, scene 2, Iago is as contemptuous of reputation as he was of virtue in the first act. He tells Cassio:

> As I am an honest man I had thought you had
> received some bodily wound; there is more sence
> in that then in Reputation. Reputation is an idle,
> and most false imposition, oft got without merit,
> and lost without deserving. You have lost no
> Reputation at all, unlesse you repute your selfe
> such a looser.

In Act III, scene 3, Iago tells Othello precisely the
opposite, as a prelude to the great persuasion scene, in
a speech of tribute to reputation which is often
quoted, almost invariably by people unaware of its hypocrisy. Iago says, preparatory to defaming Cassio
and Desdemona,

> Good name in Man, & woman (deere my
>   Lord)

Is the immediate Jewell of their Soules;
Who steales my purse, steales trash:
'Tis something, nothing;
'Twas mine, 'tis his, and has bin slave to
    thousands:
But he that filches from me my good Name,
Robs me of that, which not enriches him,
And makes me poore indeed.

By Act IV, scene 1, Othello is so much under Iago's control that such hypocrisy is no longer necessary, and Iago disparages honor (in the sense of "chastity") as ruthlessly as he had other virtues to Rodorigo and Cassio earlier. He tells Othello, in regard to Desdemona:

Her honor is an Essence that's not seene,
They have it very oft, that have it not.

Iago is just as cynical a Machiavel later in the scene, when Othello says "A Horned man's a Monster, and a Beast," and Iago replies:

Ther's many a Beast then in a populous Citty,
And many a civill Monster.

This Machiavel Iago, like the stage villain Iago discussed above, disappears after the fourth act, as though both were transient masks briefly worn by what emerges in Act V as an openly Satanic figure.

* * *

There can be no doubt of Shakespeare's awareness of the figure of the Machiavel. His references range from the most earnest use of the figure, as in *3 Henry VI*, Act III, scene 2, where the Duke of Gloucester, the future Richard III, boasts that he can "set the murtherous Machiavel to school," to the most broadly comic, as when the host of The Garter in *The Merry Wives of Windsor* asks: "Am I politic? Am I subtle? Am I a Machiavel?" The reason why an explanation of Iago's motivation in terms of the Machiavel's unprincipled greed and ruthless ambition has been so rarely advanced in Shakespeare criticism until recently is that in literal terms it explains too little of Iago's actions: the plot against Cassio might be a Machiavellian attempt as self-advancement, to replace him as lieutenant, but the plot against Desdemona is oddly pure of any possibility of a material reward. If Iago were a figure like Pedringano, a minor villain in Kyd's *The Spanish Tragedie*, soliloquizing

> Heere is the golde! This is the golde proposde!
> It is no dreame that I adventure for,
> But Pedringano is possest thereof

things would be much simpler.

What was required was a secularized theological vocabulary for converting material into immaterial rewards, and here, as with so many modern critical problems, Coleridge pioneered. If in *Lectures and Notes on Shakespere* he is still content with a "motiveless malignity" for Iago, in his later unpublished writing he tried formulating a motivation. This material has been studied by Elinor S. Shaffer and published in "Iago's Malignity Motivated: Coleridge's Unpublished 'Opus Magnum,'" in *Shakespeare Quarterly* (1968). In these late notebooks, Coleridge writes:

> If in the present work we may without impropriety refer to the work of an author next to Holy Writ the most instructive, we would add that without the perception of this truth it is impossible to understand / I might say Shakespeare generally, but more particularly / the character of Iago, who is represented as now assigning one & now another & again a third motive for his conduct, each a different motive and all alike the mere functions of his own intellectual superiority & a vicious habit of assigning the precedence or primacy to the intellectual instead of the moral; and haunted by the love of exerting power on those especially who are his superiors in moral and practical estimation. Yet how many among our modern critics have attributed to the profound author this the appropriate inconsistency of the character itself.

As Mrs. Shaffer points out, what Coleridge called "the dreadful consequences of placing the moral in subordination to the intellectual" characterizes the whole series of Shakespeare's "Machiavellian" figures: Richard III, the Bastard Falconbridge in *King John*, Edmund, and so on. As Coleridge puts it in other terms, Iago has "the dreadful habit of thinking of moral feelings and qualities only as prudential ends to means." Mrs. Shaffer sums up:

> All the characteristics, then, of the 'Machiavel' —rationality, self-interest, hypocrisy, cunning, expediency, efficiency—can be seen to fall into place under Coleridge's interpretation. Hypocrisy in particular is illuminated, and we are not surprised that Coleridge discussed it in the 'Opus Magnum' following his remarks on Iago.

What Coleridge has done, in short, is to convert the Machiavel's literal greed into Lucifer's intellectual greed, a piling up of golden outsmartings.

At the other extreme, Macaulay has given us the most literal Renaissance Italian, not specifically to explain Iago's motivation, but simply to argue the credibility of his character. Macaulay wrote in 1827, in a comment which Furness reprints:

> Many are inclined to suspect Shakespeare has been seduced into an exaggeration, and has drawn a monster who has no archetype in human nature. Now we suspect that an Italian audience, in the fifteenth century, would have felt very differently. Othello would have inspired nothing but detestation and contempt. The folly with which he trusts to the friendly professions of a man whose promotion he had obstructed,—

the credulity with which he takes unsupported assertions and trivial circumstances for unanswerable proofs,—till the exculpation can only aggravate his misery, would have excited the abhorrence and disgust of the spectators. The conduct of Iago they would assuredly have condemned; but they would have condemned it as we condemn that of his victim. Something of interest and respect would have mingled with their disapprobation. The readiness of his wit, the clearness of his judgment, the skill with which he penetrates the dispositions of others and conceals his own, would have assured to him a certain portion of their esteem.

In our century, the first account of Iago as stock Machiavel in a theatrical convention was E. E. Stoll's *Othello* (1915). The principal developers of this view of Iago as "typical elizabethan *Machiavel*" has been Wyndham Lewis in *The Lion and the Fox* (published undated, in the early 1920's). Lewis reminds us that this image was obsessive and terrifying to the Elizabethans, noting:

Mr. Edward Meyer has catalogued three hundred and ninety-five references to Machiavelli in elizabethan literature. As to his influence in England, Dr. Grosart wrote: 'I have suggested to the biographer of the renowned Machiavelli (Professor Villari of Florence) that an odd chapter might be written on the *scare* his name was for long in England: so much so that he came to be regarded as an incarnation of the Evil One himself.'

Lewis summarizes:

> Professor Bradley in his elaborate analysis of Iago says that many people have seen in Iago one of the traditional Machiavellis of the time; but he repudiates that parentage for him. Yet it hardly seems a thing about which there can be any dispute. There is no question of Shakespeare's finding this *particular* duplicity in the figure of Machiavelli. But it is certain that Iago is a variety of the recognized stage Machiavelli type. Will anyone believe that if a philosophy of duplicity and ruthless mechanical intrigue, directed to the reaching of a definite material end, had never been written by Machiavelli: if Cesare Borgia had not supplied him with a living illustration and hero . . . : and if the italian nature had not stood for intrigue, of a bold and relentless description, that Iago, the italian 'villain' of this italian story, would ever have been created?

Lewis' reading gets increasingly irresponsible and whimsical, like so much that he published, until eventually he argues against one of the most useful overstatements that Bradley ever produced, "that Iago *under no circumstances* ever tells the truth!" with the absurd "The most obvious thing about Iago is that he

gd opy

never lies, and is as open (in his villainy) as the day, as we have already said." Nevertheless, Lewis' basic contention that Iago is a Machiavel in his motivation is right and Bradley's denial of it is wrong. Lewis' view was given further currency by T. S. Eliot in "Shakespeare and the Stoicism of Seneca," where he writes:

> I think that Mr. Lewis, in the intensely interesting book mentioned, has done a real service in calling attention to the importance of Machiavelli in Elizabethan England, though this Machiavelli is only the Machiavelli of the *Contre-Machiavel*, and not in the least the real Machiavelli.

John F. Danby's *Shakespeare's Doctrine of Nature* (1948), a study of *King Lear*, pursues the image of the Machiavel in connection with Edmund, and comes up with some gradations. He distinguishes from "crude machiavellism" the "refined machiavellism" of such a figure as Prince Hal rejecting Falstaff at the end of *2 Henry IV*; in contrast, he classes Iago as the most vicious form of the phenomenon. Danby writes:

> Significantly, too, Shakespeare now blackens the machiavel more than he has ever done before. Iago has no such compunctuous visitings of nature as even Richard had, and no token repentance like Edmund's. He is a slave and a dog. The thought that he might be put to some good

use, even in the second-best world of the political, is never entertained.

Heilman in *Magic in the Web*, in accord with his pluralist emphasis ("Our principle must be *both-and;* to make Iago simply one thing or another will restrict and reduce the actual figure of the play") equivocates on the Machiavel identification as on all other exclusive readings. He writes: "Iago is a Machiavel, true; but he is something more, still fundamentally significant when the Machiavel is remembered only in footnotes; into the imitation of the maneuvers of the false friend has gone a unique intuition of human potentialities." Heilman explains later in the book: "For Shakespeare has achieved a doubleness of character which partly explains the terrifyingness of Iago, making him on the one hand a habitual, principled debunker of the nonmaterial goods of mankind, but on the other hand an intelligent perceiver of the values by which men live."

Spivack's *Shakespeare and the Allegory of Evil*, discussed in Chapter I as our principal reading of Iago in terms of the tradition of the stage villain, also touches on our present approach as "the renovation, when it occurs, of the old role by Machiavellianism in general." Spivack defines the Elizabethan stage figure with considerable eloquence:

> On their stage the Machiavellian villain, through his egoism, his ruthless energy unhampered by pious restraints, his deliberate disavowal of any

law higher than his own appetite, his penetrating and cynical awareness of the animal impulses composing man's lower nature, enacts the thrust of the new *realism* against the traditional Christian sanctities applicable to the life of this world. Legitimacy, order, honor, loyalty, love, and the stable community of human creatures under God are the easy obstacles his purposes surmount because the pieties and simplicities of *honest* men render them defenseless against his *policy*. It is a rare villain in the drama of that time who is not in some degree a Machiavel; for villainy in general, as the Elizabethans viewed and staged it, is rooted in an irreligious principle, to which the Florentine, from the same view, contributed not so much an origin as an affirmation, not so much a manifesto as a guidebook. The age was aware of Machiavellianism before it was aware of Machiavelli.

Spivack concludes that "it would not be wrong to apply the same formula to all the Shakespearian figures participating in the same hybrid convention. Neither would it be very useful." Of Iago specifically, Spivack shows the same willingness to go so far and no further. He writes:

Provided we extend the significance of the label beyond Machiavelli, since it embraces concepts of which Tudor England was conscious without the Florentine's instruction, Iago is a Machiavel. Upon the traditional pieties, as they have already been summarized, and the system of belief behind them, his derisive assault is fundamental, extending to first principles.

Spivack goes on to add:

> Labels, however, adhere only to surfaces and mock us with superficiality when we try to apply them to Shakespeare's depths. We detect the type with which he begins but lose it in the unique creation with which he ends. Applied to Iago, the Machiavellian label, while supplying some prefatory enlightenment, is too general to carry us very far into the moral meaning of his role.

Wylie Sypher's *Literature and Technology* (1968) looks at Iago in Machiavellian terms, but treats them as figurations for the socio-economic and psychological, as Coleridge treated them as figurations for the theological. Sypher writes:

> The vicious serviceable type is Iago, with his profane self-interest, blind, exploiting all idyllic relations. The gross stupidity of Iago's laissez-faire ethic is in his advice to Roderigo: put money in thy purse. This extreme puritan thrift is mere literal-mindedness, for Iago knows the price of everything and the value of nothing. His cleverness is myopia in acute form; he is sure that a good woman is fit to suckle fools, that Desdemona is full of game, that her wine is

made of grapes. This practicality is worse than cynicism because it is utterly blind to any possibility of another view of things: the facts speak for themselves. One of the psychological overtones in Iago is his joylessness, a brand of puritan deprivation or deficiency. He is lively enough, but his comedy, in spite of its resiliency, does not give pleasure—only sport. Iago remarks to Roderigo: 'If thou canst cuckold him, thou dost thyself a pleasure, me a sport.' Is it overinterpreting to find this contrast between pleasure and sport a key to Iago's comedy, which is a game played not for pleasure but for the technological skill with which moves can be made? There is something inhibited, disciplined, and parsimonious about Iago's machinations: he goes at evil-doing with a consciousness of method, a kind of gamesmanship, though he is stone blind about the reasons why the game should be played anyhow. . . . Iago's sport is an aspect of thrift: a perversion of comedy or play, which should be creative and cathartic. Iago deprives play of its ebullience, diminishes it to a technique, a shrunken puritanical strategy.

Sypher's conclusion from this is that "Iago is not truly Machiavellian, since there is no clear or beneficial intent behind his diabolism." My conclusion is that he is most transcendentally a Machiavel (along Coleridge's lines) precisely in this.

CONCLUSION

Which of these answers, then, is the real answer to the question of Iago's motivation? Does he destroy Desdemona and Othello (not to speak of Rodorigo and Æmilia) because he is a stage villain, or Satan, or an artist, or a latent homosexual, or a Machiavel? Alone, none of them is a very satisfactory answer. Together, they all are the answer, or a large part of the answer. The complexity of Iago's character, the tangle of conscious and unconscious, even conflicting, purposes suggested in him, comes from these various levels of motivation. In one of the finest pluralist criticisms of the play, *Magic in the Web*, Robert B. Heilman writes (his last words are a quotation from Maud Bodkin):

> The Magic in the Web produces a character so full and flexible that it can accommodate itself to the psychological habits of different generations. Iago may be understood as Invidia or as the Machiavel or as the Jealous Man or as the False Friend; he can be sensed at his narrowest as the villain of melodrama or at his widest as Satan— a projection of 'the forces within and without us that threaten our supreme values.'

137

The virtue of this plurality of motivations is not only to make the character rich and complex, but to add power and irony as Iago switches from one facet to another or as the audience becomes aware of one stratum underlying another. I do not want to do my reader's work for him in putting together these five readings and allowing them to interplay, but an example or two may be useful in demonstrating how such interplay functions. There is a good case of this in the play's first scene, in the start of the heart-on-the-sleeve speech quoted several times in earlier chapters:

> Were I the Moore, I would not be Iago:
> In following him, I follow but my selfe.
> Heaven is my Judge, not I for love and dutie,
> But seeming so, for my peculiar end.

I have in various places pointed out that the first two lines seem only stage-villain revelations until they are realized to be a Satanic irony, culminating in "Heaven is my Judge"; that "not I for love," coming after "In following him, I follow but my selfe" (that is, my own nature), gives us a sudden flash of the latent homosexual; that "But seeming so, for my peculiar end" returns us to the stage villain, but now the face behind his mask is the author's own, falsifying for *his* peculiar end. The effect of these alternating aspects, and aspects behind aspects, in four lines is to pack the speech with tension, paradox, and irony.

The richest example of this reinforcement in the whole play, perhaps, is the single line, not so far quoted in this book, which ends the scene in which Othello and Iago kneel and make their dreadful pact together. Carried away, Othello says, "Now art thou my Lieutenant," and Iago replies with passion, "I am your owne for ever." This is simultaneously a pinnacle of duplicity for the stage villain, Satan's revelation of Othello's eternal damnation, William Shakespeare's oath of fealty to his own imaginative creation, the repressed homosexual's marriage vow, and the Machiavel's veiled boast that he is now not servant but master. No wonder the line seems so resonant.

Any single critical method, limited by its own terminology to making only certain observations, is thus inevitably reductive and partial. The assumption of pluralist criticism is that a number of such radically different approaches will produce a richer and more complex understanding of the imaginative work than any single approach could. In pluralist terms, all of these methods are equal, cooperating partners in a critical symposium. But the pressures (in the critic's own set of values, in what seems to be the emphasis of the work) are very great to turn this democratic equality into a hierarchical structure, where one terminology is central and all others radiate out from it. Spivack did that with the tradition of the Vice, making it *the* essence of Iago and his true motivation, and handling all other theories of motivation (where he did not simply reject them) as developments or adaptations of the Vice. Lewis did the same thing much less formally with the Machiavel, at various times identifying Iago with David slaying Goliath and with Charlie Chaplin winning through, but always seeing them as transformations of his basic figure. Kenneth Burke, were he to venture this sort of pluralist reading, would make symbolic action (in a larger and more complex sense than mine in the third chapter) the hub, and handle all the other meanings as spokes radiating out from that.

This raises the question of what sort of hierarchy I would construct were I required to arrange these readings hierarchically. The answer, I suspect, is that the theological reading would be my hub in this case. For me, the figuration of Satan (in a triad with figurations of Judas and Christ) is Iago's richest and most resonant meaning. The stage villain and the Machiavel tend to disappear before the fifth act, as noted above, as they become with increasing clarity more-or-less ingratiating masks for Satan. The Freudian latent homosexual, a type which includes us all, surely has nothing Satanic about it, but the specific nature of Iago's case, unconscious love warped into the most terrible and implacable hate, is Satanic, is in fact the pattern of Lucifer's Fall. As for the figure of the artist, our remaining reading, in the deepest perspective we can recognize that at the beginning of *The Tempest* Prospero finds the world in the hands of the demons, and by his divine creative powers, reorders chaos, defeats the demons, and restores order and justice. In this perspective, as one or two commentators have observed, he is God—and it is easy enough to

add the corollary that if Iago is Satan, then Shakespeare's full portrait of the artist, extending both figures to their ultimates, is as god-devil.

Yet the essential weakness of hierarchical criticism,
however tempting, is that it is ultimately more reductive than pluralist criticism. As C. L. Barber has written to me in a private communication:

> . . . no one vocabulary is controlling because
> the final control is the control of tragic form;
> the vocabularies of interpretation merge into one
> another . . . ; as this happens, they merge into
> the whole which is the play, the whole which
> controls them as aspects of itself. So with Desde-
> mona: she is felt as a type of Christ, her death a
> heavy hour when the affrighted globe should
> yawn at alteration; but she is also a woman
> lying in her marriage bed on her wedding
> sheets, and after her 'resurrection' and its for-
> giving gesture, she's dead as earth, there is no
> Promethean heat that can relume her light. Talk
> about the integrity of the work of art became
> obsessive in some New Criticism; but the fact
> remains, awkward as it is for us villainous
> critics who want to entrap the play in our webs.

Theodore Spencer, in *Shakespeare and the Nature of
Man* (1942), made the same point in connection with
The Tempest: "But the play itself, like all of Shakespeare's work, like human life, defies any scheme so
neat and so mechanical." Frank Prentice Rand gave us

essentially the same warning in "The Over Garrulous Iago" in *Shakespeare Quarterly* (1950), reminding us that "if the play is to be anything more than a parable, we must feel that it represents conflict between, and within, actual human beings." It is Barber's formally controlled whole, Spencer's defiance of the schematic, Rand's human actuality, which seem safer in the hands of pluralist criticism, with its built-in self-correction and emphasis on dialectic interplay and enrichment of each limited approach, than in the hands of any single critical method considered as *the* method or *the* central method, and thus inevitably overstated.

A brief word must be said about Othello's motivation, along with Shakespeare's and the audience's. In the old Freudian readings, of which Freud on *Hamlet*, expanded by Jones, is the classic example, life was simple: the mechanism running the play was an Oedipus complex which was unconscious in Hamlet, unconscious in Shakespeare, and unconscious in each member of the audience or reader (at least in each such hearer or reader who got caught up in the play emotionally). Alas, this is a little too simple for these less innocent times. The question of consciousness in Shakespeare and the audience will be taken up below. Here I should like to handle Othello's motivation (which might be the subject for a comparable book) only in the most cursory fashion. It is impossible to avoid noticing that his vulnerability to Iago's blandishments is extraordinary, that all his trust in Desdemona collapses with lightning rapidity. As J. I. M.

Stewart reminds us, Iago tells four people (the other three are Rodorigo, Cassio, and Æmilia) that Desdemona is unfaithful, but only Othello believes him. Heilman asks: "What is there in the first place that makes Othello corrode so easily?" It is hard to avoid the conclusion that Shakespeare has drawn an answering latent homosexuality in Othello which responds readily to Iago's (this is not to slight such obvious motivations on the surface of the play as his being a Moor, his late marriage into an unfamiliar world, and such).

There is a neat example of the difference between tragedy and comedy in the contrast of the way the matter of suspicion is handled in *Othello* and in Nicholas Udall's comedy *Ralph Roister Doister*. In the course of the latter's action, Gawyn Goodlucke comes to suspect the fidelity of his betrothed, Christian Custance, because of evidence of her suspicious behavior brought to him by his trusted man Sym Suresby. When he announces this evidence, Sym adds:

Sir, though I to you be a servant true and just,
Yet doe not ye therfore your faithfull spouse mystrust;
But examine the matter, and if ye shall it finde
To be all well, be not ye for my wordes unkinde.

If we can imagine Iago making such a speech in full honesty, all our tragedy would fly out the window as good comic common sense flew in.

Which, somewhat deviously, brings us to the question of Shakespeare's consciousness of the meanings and motivations which have been the subject of this book. I would take Furness' position (and I have come to it reluctantly over the years, as he did) that just about every effect in Shakespeare is conscious. I am defining "consciousness" as I. A. Richards does in his celebrated "Definition of a Poem" in Chapter 30 of *Practical Criticism:* "the relevant experience of the poet when contemplating the completed composition." It is not at all a matter of his antecedent intention: for all we know (although it does not seem too likely in terms of our sense of his nature and style), Shakespeare may have written in a kind of trance state, as have a number of poets since. What the artist is conscious of is what he can see (or, better, experience) as he reads over the completed composition. This goes for Shakespeare's celebrated Oedipus complex too. Freud named it the "Oedipus" complex to credit not only Sophocles but the creator of *Hamlet* (and writers generally) with always having known about such matters, with having discovered them essentially as he did, by careful study of oneself and others; he cannot then turn around in his *Hamlet* discussion and make all this unconscious in Shakespeare.

The plays make it equally clear that Shakespeare knew at least as much as Anna Freud about the defense mechanisms; even Hamlet's mother was something of an ego psychologist in observing, "The lady doth protest too much, methinks." In general, I differ from all the Freudians I have read in assuming Shakespeare as a knowing depth psychologist. This is not to say that he had no unconscious, or that nothing in his writings escaped his recognition; only that his area of unconsciousness was minimal. I would imagine, for example, that the famous cluster of images discovered by Walter Whiter, the fawning-dog-licking-melting-candy, each term of which seems to call up all the others in contexts of treachery and betrayal, was unconscious, since its communicative logic is so slight; that is, I think: if Shakespeare had noticed the association he would have emended it.

That said, we can discuss the specific question of Shakespeare's conscious awareness of these five dimensions of motivation in Iago. He was obviously aware of the tradition of the stage villain, and made deliberate use of it in Iago's asides and soliloquies. The parallel with Satan, Judas, and Christ is carefully written in, as the "base Judean" simile makes clear. The latent homosexuality must be conscious, since the evidence for it is not in Cinthio but has all been added by Shakespeare, and since homosexual and bisexual themes are so overt in other of his plays and in the *Sonnets*. As for Shakespeare's deliberately making Iago a Machiavel, we have only to recall that his world was saturated with the image (or the distorted image) of Machiavelli, and that a number of his other villains—certainly Richard, Edmund, Falconbridge, and Aaron the Moor—also reflect that figure. The best case for unconsciousness is in Iago as a self-portrait, where there is little overt comparison with the artist or other direct evidence. The inclusion of Prospero, however, makes the identification much likelier, since in *The Tempest* the comparison *is* overt (at least "art" is the constant word for Prospero's magic). Beyond that, to assume that we can recognize Iago plotting like a playwright, or rhyming like a hired poet, and that Shakespeare could not, is absurd on the face of it. The beginning of critical humility is the assumption that anything which we (or Halliwell, or Bradley, or Spivack) can see in the plays, Shakespeare could see too, and that anything in the text which works on us was deliberately put (or left) in the text to work as it does.

This raises the more interesting, but unfortunately unanswerable, question of the Elizabethan audience's awareness of these meanings and motivations. First, the Elizabethan audience was unusually differentiated; it ranged from Shakespeare's fellow poets and playwrights to drunken tinkers. Taking a representative sober auditor with some education as the mean, we can try an enlightened guess at his awareness: he would recognize, and enjoy, the stage villainy; he would be sharply aware of the Christian parallel, for which all the emblematic literature and typological sermons of his time had prepared him; he would probably not notice the portrait of the artist; he would most likely respond only on an unconscious level to the latent homosexuality; he would recognize, perhaps as primary, the Machiavel. In short: "A play with a damned villainous Italian, wicked as the betrayers of our Lord, very tragic and full of most excellent ranting."

Conclusion

We might end, where we began, with the epigraph on the title page, spoken by Iago in an effort to persuade Desdemona not to force him to extemporise. It, too, translates into all five vocabularies, and it is additionally useful in reminding us that critics, too, can sometimes be most ingenious villains.

APPENDIX

BY
PHOEBE PETTINGELL

APPENDIX

*Jago's motivation in Arrigo Boito's libretto
and Giuseppe Verdi's music for the opera*
Otello

> *Beltà ed amor in dolce inno concordi.*
> *I vostri infrangerò soavi accordi.*

BEAUTY and love, united in sweet concert," sings
Jago, "I will shatter your gentle harmonies."
Both Boito and Verdi were aware that the central action of Shakespeare's play consisted of the shattering
of these harmonies. The opera *Otello* shows Jago setting "down the pegs" as his serpentine dissonances
gradually disintegrate the melodious love of the Moor
and Desdemona.

Verdi's *Otello* is perhaps nearly as well known to-
day as Shakespeare's play, and it is almost universally
believed that the opera is a remarkably faithful adaptation. Most nineteenth-century operas purporting to
derive from Shakespeare were catastrophes. Ambroise
Thomas ended his *Hamlet* with the hero being ac-
claimed King of Denmark, while Charles Gounod's
Roméo et Juliette showed the lovers expiring in each
other's arms in the midst of a duet, with no subsequent reconciliation of the families. One of Verdi's
first successful operas was *Macbeth* (1847, revised in

1865), reasonably faithful to Shakespeare, but marred by a poor libretto. He was therefore initially wary, even after Boito showed him a preliminary sketch for *Otello*, and hesitated to commit himself to the project, especially since an earlier opera on the subject by Rossini had been unsuccessful. But Boito was an excellent translator, as well as a poet and a composer in his own right; his opera *Mefistofele* is still the most faithful adaptation of Goethe's *Faust*. Faced with the problem of condensing approximately 3500 lines in Shakespeare's play to something fewer than 800 for a four-act opera, Boito needed to increase the pace. Taking his cue from classical drama, he eliminated Shakespeare's first act, thus narrowing the action to Cyprus, and he included the vital material lost by the cut, in a love duet between Otello and Desdemona ("She loved me for the dangers I had passed"). But there was still the necessity of making the already rapid disintegration of the marriage even more rapid, and Boito accomplished this through his treatment of Jago, adapting the character to his purposes, while trying not to do violence to Shakespeare's conception.

In the play, Iago is given the opportunity to soliloquize on the momentary rationalizations for his mode of action. Boito simply did not have the space for many of these; furthermore, when lines are sung, one cannot depend on the audience understanding all the words. Therefore, the libretto deletes such details as Iago's suspicion of Othello's and Cassio's adultery with Emilia as unnecessary: in the first place, Shakespeare suggests that Iago does not even believe it himself; secondly, an Italian audience might interpret it as ample motivation for all Iago's plots, thus making the opera into a double revenge and murder story. Instead, Boito supplied an aria in which Jago expresses his system of values. Although not in the play, the text is derived from Shakespearian sources, perhaps most obviously the Bastard's speech from *King Lear:* "Thou, nature, art my goddess; to thy law my services are bound." Jago's "Credo" is well worth a careful examination, as it displays in miniature most of Boito's conceptions of this character:

Credo in un Dio crudel che m'ha creato
simile a sè e che nell'ira io nomo.
Dalla viltà d'un germe o d'un atomo
vile son nato.
Son scellerato perchè son uomo;
e sento il fango originario in me.
Si! quest'è la mia fè!
Credo con fermo cuor,
siccome crede la vedovella al tempio,
che il mal ch'io penso e che da ma procede,
per il mio destino adempio.
Credo che il giusto è un istrion beffardo
e nel viso e nel cuor,
che tutto è in lui bugiardo:
lagrima, bacio, sguardo,
sacrificio ed onor.

E credo l'uom giuoco d'iniqua sorte
dal germe della culla
al verme dell'avel.
Vien dopo tanta irrision la Morte.
E poi? e poi?
La Morte è il Nulla.
È vecchia fola il Ciel.

"I believe in one God, cruel, who has created me in his own image, and whose name I cry in hate. From the vileness of some germ or atom, vile was I born. I am wicked because I am a man, and I can feel the primal evil in me. Yes, I believe this. I believe with as firm a heart as does the widow in church, that every evil thought which comes from me fulfills my destiny. I believe that the just man is a jesting 'ham' in both appearances and feelings, and that everything about him lies: tears, kisses, glances, his sacrifices, and his honor. And I believe man to be the sport of evil fortune from the germ of the cradle to the worm of the grave. And after all this mockery comes Death. And then? then? Death is annihilation, and Heaven is a fable."

On the simplest level, Jago is expressing himself in the conventional tones of the stage villain in telling the audience that he is a wicked man who intends to behave wickedly. His first appearance in the opera is to announce the loss of the mainsail on Otello's ship, which reveals him as a bearer of bad news; his next line, expressing a wish that the ship sink, betrays the villain, as the fact that he is a baritone has already led the audience to suspect. Throughout the opera, Jago indulges in villainous asides, "Inferno e morte!" "Il mio velen lavora" ("My poison works,") and so on. He lies blatantly to the other characters, describing himself to Roderigo as "amico tuo sincero," protesting his overwhelming love to Otello, and his solicitude to Desdemona. At the end of the third act, Otello has fallen unconscious, and, while the unsuspecting crowds outside are cheering him, Jago asks rhetorically, "Chi può vietar che questa fronte prema col mio tallone?"—"Who can prevent me from grinding his forehead beneath my heel?"—a revelation of evil triumph unsurpassed in opera. By the time of the composition of *Otello*, the name "Jago" was already a catchword for villain. In Puccini's *Tosca*, the wicked chief of police, Scarpia, hatching a plot, remarks, "Jago used a handkerchief; I will use a fan."

Most crucially, of course, the Credo is a blasphemous Satanic parody of "Credo in unum Deum," the basic statement of faith of the Christian Church. As the Nicene Creed speaks of Christ as the only begotten Son, of the same substance (*homoousion* in Greek, *consubstantialem* in Latin) as His Father, so Jago claims to be of "il fango originario" of his creator, and to follow his will in spreading confusion. With the Marcionites, Jago believes that Satan created the world; unlike them, he worships that creator, and often speaks of himself in Satanic terms. In the first act, he tells Roderigo, "Se un fragil voto di femmina non è tropp'arduro nodo pel genio mio nè per l'inferno, giuro che quella donna serà tua." "If a woman's fragile vow is not too hard a problem for my wit or for Hell, I promise that you shall have this lady." As Cassio goes to greet Desdemona, Jago says, "Ti spinge il tuo dimone, e il tuo dimon son io." "Your demon drives you on, and I am that demon." Later, seeing Cassio and Desdemona strolling together, the demon prays, "Aiuta Satana il mio cimento," a prayer which is immediately answered as Otello appears. But in the monstrous oath at the end of the second act, it is Otello who uses hellish imagery, "Per la morte e per l'oscuro mar sterminator . . . d'ira e d'impeto tremendo"—"By death and by the dark and boundless sea . . . with rage and great vehemence"—while Jago ironically swears by the sun which enlivens all creation. Since the "Credo" shows that he believes that the world is in the hands of the demons, this oath carries a different tone to the audience than it does to Otello. But, in general, as Jago gains possession of Otello's soul, we hear the demonic voice speaking more out of Otello than out of Jago, as when the Moor cries out from the depths of his agony, for damnation, ruin, and death. Others recognize Jago's diabolic role. Roderigo admits, "t'ho venduto onore e fè." "I have sold you my honor and my faith," in short, a Satanic pact. When Jago snatches the handkerchief from Emilia, she refers to his "artigli truci" ("cruel talons") as though he were physically an incarnate devil. Finally, a fine demonic touch is added to Jago's character as he denies Otello an explanation of his motivation for lying, after the murder of Desdemona and the discovery of his plot, with the single word, "No!" Boito's Mefistofele had defined himself as "lo spirito che nega"—"the spirit who denies"—and Jago, who has been true to his Satanic nature, ends with an ultimate negation.

Apparently Boito did not recognize the Judas imagery which Shakespeare used for Otello, but he certainly perceived Desdemona's heavenly role. However, he associated her with the Virgin more than with Christ. Desdemona becomes the Merciful Intercessor, a role which Roman Catholics tend to associate with Mary, as Protestants and Anglicans associate it with Jesus. Otello's love for his wife and his description of her nature are perilously close to *latria*, the devotion due to saints and to the Mother of God. He tells her, "Ingentilia di lagrime la storia il tuo bel viso e il labbro di sospir; scendean sulle mie tenebre la gloria, il paradiso e gli astri a benedir." "The tears on your beautiful face and the sighs from your lips refined my story. On my darkness descended glory, paradise, and the blessing of heaven." He refers to her marriage to him as "quest'attimo divino," and he looks on her as on the Grace of Heaven. At the mere suggestion that she may be unfaithful he cries out, "S'ella m'inganna, il ciel sè stesso irride!" "If she be false, then heaven mocks itself." Later, in an appalling image, Otello describes "Rose-lipped Mercy" as covering "il tuo viso santo coll'orrida larva infernal!"—"Your holy face with the horrid shadow of hell." This is meant to describe Mercy turning into Vengeance for the murder of Desdemona, but it is also Otello's image of the corruption of his saint into a devil. In the Council Chamber scene, he calls her "my demon," and at the end, so much identifies her with his image of Heaven corrupted that he cries out as he strikes her, "Anima mia, ti maledico!"—"My soul, I curse you!" This interpretation was anticipated by Coleridge when he wrote that "Othello has no life but in Desdemona; the belief that she, his angel, had fallen from the heaven of her native innocence, wrought a civil war in his heart." When, after the murder, Emilia reveals Desdemona's complete innocence, Otello addresses the corpse of his wife as "pia creatura" ("saintly creature") and describes her as "in cielo assorta." Since, in Catholic doctrine the Virgin is believed to have ascended directly to Heaven, because she was without sin, Otello is, in effect, identifying Desdemona with Mary as being entirely pure. Desdemona earlier identifies herself as the Loving Intercessor when she tells her husband, "Io prego il cielo per te con questo pianto." "I implore Heaven for you with these tears."

Other personages in the opera also regard Desdemona as a figuration of Mary. Cyprus is especially associated with the cult of the Virgin, and the Cypriots make this allusion when they offer Desdemona "il giglio soave stel / che in man degl'angeli fu assunto in ciel / che abbella il fulgido manto e la gonna / della Madonna e il santo vel"—"The sweet lily which the angels carried in their hands to heaven, which decorates the shining mantel and gown and the holy veil of the Madonna." They also compare their new lady to "un immagine sacra" ("a sacred image") and later, when Otello has struck her in the Council Chamber scene, the ladies observe, "Piangon così nel ciel lor pianto gli angeli quando perduto giace il peccator." "Her weeping is like the tears of the angels when a sinner lies lost." The cult of Mary in the Middle Ages believed that the Queen of Heaven was so tender-hearted that she often interceded with her Son for sinners justifiably damned (an example of the Marcionite heresy, "Love frees from the Law").

Even objects associated with Desdemona take on her properties. Although Cassio does not know that the handkerchief he has discovered in his room is hers, he describes it as "Miracolo vago" ("lovely miracle") and "tessuta dall'aure del ciel," "of the texture of heaven's breezes," not unlike the phrases which he uses to describe Desdemona herself. Even Jago refers to her (albeit mockingly) as "la via di salvazione," but perhaps he is not mocking, for, as a creature of hell, he doubtless knows that she is saved and saves while he is damned.

After Desdemona dismisses Emilia and says farewell to her, as if foreseeing her death, she kneels down to recite the "Ave Maria" for all souls, the very image of the Mother of Sorrows, interceding with her archetype out of her own infinite love. When confronted by Otello and asked to confess her sin, she replies, "My sin is love," and although, to the warped mind of the

Moor, this seems a confession of her adultery with Cassio, she means that pure love is sinless. At last, she becomes truly Christlike as she asks Otello, "E perchè t'amo m'uccidi?" "Will you kill me because I love you?" This heartbreaking question echoes the famous passage from Micah (6:3), a part of the Good Friday service in the Catholic Church, where Christ asks from the Cross, "Oh my people, what have I done to thee? And wherein have I wearied thee?" as He reminds them of His Love.

In one aspect, Jago as the Devil, and Desdemona as the Madonna, battle over the soul of Everyman—Otello. Long before the murder, Otello's soul suffers torments. When Jago tells Otello that he will overhear Cassio revealing his involvement with Desdemona, the Moor exclaims, "Cielo! O gioia! Orror! Supplizî immondi!" as though he had just realized the full extent of his damnation. But at the end, as he kisses Desdemona's corpse, recalling the ecstasy of their first love, his suffering is over. Perhaps, like the medieval monk Theophilus, who sold his soul to the devil but was redeemed by Christ's compassion at the tears of His Mother, Otello, too, in Boito's libretto, is snatched from the mouth of Hell, in spite of his double guilt of murder and suicide, by Desdemona's sacrificial death for love.

Boito has drawn other mythological parallels in the opera, neither Christian nor Shakespearian. Jago is a form of the Trickster, a minor god, best exemplified in opera by Wagner's Loge in *Das Rheingold*. As

Loge, the fire god, watches Wotan and the others cross the Rainbow Bridge to Walhalla, he tells the audience that, although for the present he is on the side of the gods (as earlier he had been on the side of the Rhinemaidens) he may turn against them and destroy them. In *Die Walküre*, we find that Wotan has changed Loge back into his original element, and tamed him, but in *Die Götterdämmerung*, Loge's fire destroys Walhalla and the gods. Otello is ostensibly more powerful than Jago, who pretends to be his servant, but, when the time comes, the clever servant is able to throw off his disguise and appear as master, as he plants a triumphant foot upon the head of the fallen hero. The identifying mark of the Trickster is that he poses as something that he is not, in this case as a bluff, honest, faithful soldier, and then, when he is put in a position of trust, outwits his superiors.

There is still another identification of the three principal characters: with pagan gods. This identification does not run throughout the opera, but is only in evidence at the beginning, and is heavily overlaid with Christian resonance. In the drinking scene, Jago becomes a malign Bacchus, befuddling the wits of Cassio and the Cypriots to provoke a riot. Shortly afterwards, Otello and Desdemona, after having reestablished peace, sing their duet, while in the sky "Venere splende." Earlier, on Otello's first entrance, he rejoiced at the downfall of the enemy, identifying himself as the triumphant warrior, Desdemona's "superbo guerrier." The lovers are in fact, briefly, Mars

and Venus, he the invincible in battle, she the personification of love. The cult of the Virgin on Cyprus was,
in pre-Christian times, the cult of Aphrodite, and
Desdemona, as the island's most beautiful treasure,
embodies both the goddess and the Madonna, as Jago
is both Bacchus and Satan. By the second act, Otello
forswears his military triumphs and abandons himself
to despair and revenge, and by the third act Desdemona has become the Suffering Servant.

In all fairness, it must be confessed that nineteenth
century opera compares its heroines to heavenly beings, and its villains to demonic ones, with considerable frequency, and that, in general, its librettists use
religious imagery for which Shakespeare or his seventeenth century contemporaries would have been
summoned before the Star Chamber. In Verdi's own
operas, the seduced and abandoned Gilda of *Rigoletto*
and the *demi-mondaine* Violetta of *La Traviata* both
describe themselves on their deathbeds as interceding
angels, though they are far from the "casto altare" to
which the Cypriots compare Desdemona. There is a
baroque sentimentality in modern Italian culture,
which mixes sacred and secular in a fashion alien to
Shakespeare and the English temperament (the naming of a sweetish white wine *Lacrimi Cristi* is a fair
example). Nonetheless, it is as unfair to accuse such a
careful and meticulous artist as Boito of this fault as it
would be to accuse Dante. In *Mefistofele*, Boito was
faithful to the more orthodox of Goethe's religious
views, and while he adapted *Otello* slightly for an

Italian audience, he showed a skillful and sensitive awareness of Shakespeare's own imagery and purposes.

Closely related to the Satanism in the "Credo" is its Machiavellianism. When Jago says, "Son scellerato perche son uomo"—"I am wicked because I am a man" —he is expressing the paradoxical view that since man's nature is base, he is indeed "onesto Jago" in acting on these principles, while a man like Otello, bound by principles of honor, is "un istrion beffardo." Some of Jago's advice is worthy of a student of *Il Principe*. He tells Roderigo, "Ma com'é ver che tu Roderigo sei, così è pur vero che se il Moro io fossi vedermi non vorrei d'attorno un Jago." "But as it is certain that you are Roderigo, it is equally certain that if I were the Moor, I should not like to have an Jago around me." In other words, a shrewd man ought to make sure that his servants have no grudges against him. Jago also tells the young man that his hatred for both Otello and Cassio stems from bitterness about being passed over for the post of lieutenant. Later he advises Roderigo in his own self-interest to kill Cassio, thus prolonging Desdemona's stay in Cyprus. However, this Machiavellianism is only another of Jago's poses: he does not seem to care when he finally gets Cassio's place, and his advice to Roderigo is all lies. Jago is much more the Machiavel of Gentillet's *Contre-Machiavel*, who works, not for his self-interest, but for the pure joy of destroying, and witnessing the suffering of others. This Machiavel revels in the breakdown of order:

while the crowds outside the governor's palace ac-
claim Otello as the "Leon di Venezia!" Jago points to
the prone General and mocks, "Ecco il Leone!" Thus,
what delights him about Otello's fall has gone beyond
the personal to the symbolic—Otello as a symbol of
the state, of honor and glory, brought lower than a
beast.

As has been shown on p. 129, Macaulay believed
that an Italian Renaissance audience would have felt
toward Iago as an English audience feels toward
Othello: a flawed man, but admirable. In support of
this supposition, there is a letter written by Blanche
Roosevelt to Wilkie Collins after the world premiere
of *Otello* in Rome, describing Victor Maurel, the
French baritone who created the role of Jago. Miss
Roosevelt writes:

> He entered at once into the fullest sympathies of
> the audience, and I could not help then and
> there contrasting the Iagos we have seen in other
> countries with the Iagos we always see in Italy.
> Iago even seems a *persona grata* to the public;
> the qualities which raise a thrill of horror in the
> righteous Anglo-Saxon are received by this sus-
> ceptible nation with placid contentment and
> relief. His vileness, ruses, and perfidy are ac-
> cepted for their art, not their nature; his in-
> genious devices cause heartfelt plaudits; and
> let me add that never will you hear a gallery
> god in Italy express any disapprobation with a

successful knave. Had Iago not succeeded, there is every reason to believe that *Othello* would have been left out of the Italian Shakespearean repertory. On noting his more than prominence in this opera . . . I could well understand Boito's and Verdi's inclination to call their work *Iago* and not *Othello*. Iago is essentially Italian, not in the sense of vice, but of artistic villainy: he reasons from the personal standpoint, and his reasons find a universal echo in the land which gave birth to such a student of nature as Machiavelli. Othello, you will see, is an inferior creature, and plays an inferior part.

In this shrewd analysis, Miss Roosevelt observes that it is the perspective of knavery as art, not life, which causes the Italian audience to admire Jago, and this perspective casts a new light on the "Credo." Boito seems to have conceived of it as simply one more of Jago's rationalizations, and *not* the final word on his behavior (a fact which has escaped most commentators). It is an attempt to convince the audience of his value system as an apology for his acts, or, if not to convince them, at least to make them understand why he is what he is—and as such is an artistic *tour de force.*

As artist, Jago, besides engineering the plot, as in Shakespeare, develops a metaphor for his machinations, only suggested in the play. On first securing the handkerchief from Emilia, he remarks, "Con questi fili tramerò la prova del peccato d'amor," which is adapted from Shakespeare's "With as little a web as this, will I ensnare as great a fly as Cassio." Later Jago amplifies this further when he jokingly warns Cassio of the handkerchief, "Questa è una ragna dove il tuo cuor casca, si lagna, s'impiglia e muor." "It is a spider web into which your heart falls, cries out, is enmeshed, and dies." In this imagery, Jago's poison, to which he several times refers, is the toxin which the spider injects into its already captured prey, and his jubilation at the end of the Council Chamber scene is that of the spider having finally subdued its victim.

In contrast to the image of the artist as a destructive monster, Jago's image for Otello is of a self-destructive creature, first given in the speech on Jealousy. Boito wisely decided not to wrestle with the confused and confusing text regarding the "green-eyed monster" and rewrote the passage: "È un'idra fosca, livida, cieca, col suo veleno sè stessa attosca, vivida piaga le squarcia il seno." "It is a dusky hydra, bruised and blind, poisoning itself with its own venom, its breast rent with a great wound." Alas, we see its appropriateness for Otello all too well; his first reaction to the news of Desdemona's supposed infidelity is to find fault with himself: he is uncivilized, he is old, he is black; no wonder Desdemona prefers others. In the Council Chamber scene, the courtiers describe him as tearing his breast with his nails. At one point, he cries out in despair, "Fuggirmi io sol non so!" "I cannot escape from myself." Once the spider has poisoned him,

Otello drives himself mad, and only through the jar-
ring events at the end can he regain his sanity and free
himself from the chimeras which Jago has conjured
up.

Finally, after the image of director-playwright, and
spider-stage manager, we come to the evil musician,
the destroyer of harmonies whom we mentioned at the
beginning. We shall have more opportunity to examine this role in the discussion of Verdi's music.

Too much has been made of Boito's fidelity to
Shakespeare. Translations of the libretto have borrowed lines from the play and harmonized differences;
the poet made a classical drama out of an English Renaissance play, thus changing its scope. We have seen
how Boito adapted the play's imagery to his own ends.
He seems to have been unconsciously aware of Iago's
latent homosexuality, because most of the signs of it in
the play are omitted in the opera—the embrace in Cassio's dream, the oath to be Othello's "own forever,"
and the vulgar jokes about women. Such stage business as Booth's hand-kissing might well go unnoticed
by an Italian audience, with a more permissive attitude about physical demonstrativeness between men.
But if Boito was not faithful to the text of the play, he
was constant to Shakespeare's purposes. It would have
been easy to give Jago simple motivations—to return
to Cinthio for instance—but Boito resisted these impulses. He, too, was nothing if not critical, preserving
the central structure of the play, rendering the lines
into his admirable Italian verse, and retaining the
complexities which give *Othello* its interest. Of this

adaptation, it can truly be said that the letter killeth, but the spirit giveth life.

So far, we have only discussed one aspect of the opera, although it is somewhat easier to speak with certainty about words than about music. Without the music, however, the libretto would have no purpose, so that it will be necessary to reconstruct Verdi's own conception of Jago beyond his tacit acceptance of Boito's text. Francis Toye, in his biography *Giuseppi Verdi: His Life and Works*, quotes from a letter in which the composer describes the kind of man who could, in his opinion, deceive so many:

> If I were an actor and had to act Iago, I should like to portray rather a sparse, tall man with thin lips, small eyes set close together like a monkey's, a high receding forehead, and a head well developed at the back. His manner should be vague, nonchalant, indifferent to everything, skeptical, pungent. He should throw off good and evil sentiments lightly, as if he were thinking of something quite different from his actual utterances. Thus, if somebody reproached him, saying: 'What you propose is infamous,' he would reply, 'Really? . . . I did not think it was . . . don't let us talk about it anymore.' A man like this might deceive anybody, even his own wife to a certain extent.

The Motivation of Verdi's Jago

Verdi seems to have seen Jago as a Satanic figure, disguising his evil behind a mask of frivolity. (It will be noticed that his description of careless trifling closely resembles that of the role as played by the elder Booth.)

Jago's music is suave and rough by turns, but always menacing. The "Brindisi" or Drinking Song, which Jago uses to seduce Cassio into quarrelsome drunkenness, is a manifestation of one part of his character. "Brindisis" are standard set pieces in nineteenth-century opera, but this one is cleverly incorporated into the action, as well as revealing Jago's duplicity. *Othello* contains two songs, "And let me the canakin clink," sung by Iago, and Desdemona's "Willow Song." Each is integral to the play's movement, and each was developed into an aria in the opera. The vocal line of the "Brindisi" is very long, extended and distorted against the rhythm, suggesting a Bacchic abandon. Jago also uses a peculiar apoggiatura (grace note) which gives a slight twist to what he is saying.

The minor key and the distorted rhythm reinforce the tension of the song, as Jago repeats the extended "Beva," his voice descending an octave by half steps, as if musically portraying the fall which Cassio's drunkenness will precipitate.

As Cassio becomes progressively inebriated, his speech becomes blurred, and Jago's sharp stacatto notes undercut the tenor's voice until he breaks off in confusion.

This undercutting is a device of Jago's. In Act II, as Desdemona and the Cypriots sing of beauty and love, the baritone's voice can be detected beneath their melody, plotting the untuning of their harmonies. Again, in the Council Chamber scene, while Desdemona, Cassio, Lodovico, Emilia, and the chorus sing of their shock and horror at the events, Jago can be heard conspiring with Otello and Roderigo.

Although Jago's music so far has revealed his twisted and subtle duplicity, it is not until the introduction to the "Credo" that the music reveals his Satanic nature. The parallel octaves create an empty sound, disapproved of in traditional harmony because of their peculiar effect. Verdi has used this effect to its utmost advantage here.

The grace note at the end of the phrase, Jago's signature, resolves into a tremolo acting as an "objective correlative" for the twisted derisive hate he feels for the world.

As Jago's music is demonic, Desdemona's is fittingly angelic, from the serenity of the love duet to the moving accents of the "Willow Song," suggestive of weeping, and the quiet meditative tone of the "Ave Maria." Her greeting to the Cypriots is of surpassing beauty, so that not only Otello, but the audience, is deeply moved by her perfect innocence.

The playful apoggiatura, emphasizing the word "danza," causes the melodic line to dance also. In contrast, Jago breaks the deceptively suave line of "Era la notte" ("Cassio's dream") with an inappropriate grace note, placed on the word "mutò" ("silent"), which twists the seemingly innocent narrative into an emphasis which will drive Otello mad.

in cie co le - tar - go si mu - tò.

This apoggiatura becomes another of Jago's Machiavel devices.

Jago's music emphasizes another aspect of Satan: the Eden serpent. His description of the Hydra of Jealousy

insinuates itself into Otello's brain, and into the prelude to Act III, twisting its way from bass to the treble in the orchestra. Soon the monster has overtaken the Moor, and in his aria "Dio! mi potevi scagliar tutti i mali della miseria" ("Lord, the mightiest have hurled upon me all ills and misery") he admits that with his faith in Desdemona destroyed, he has lost all hope. The music accurately portrays this heartbreaking despair

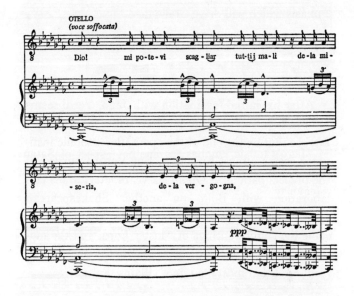

with the sobbing triplet figures repeated in the orchestra, and the descending octaves (reminiscent of the "Credo"). As Jago scarcely appears in the fourth act, his twisted music must take root in Otello to drive him on to the murder. Only afterwards does the orchestra recapture the ecstasy of the love duet, as Otello kills himself to die upon a kiss, and the sweet concert which Jago has disrupted returns for the last time.

After his initial fascination with Jago, Verdi seems to have been increasingly involved with Otello's tragic fate, so that by the end of the opera, the demonic instigator seems almost forgotten. But Verdi returned to the preoccupations of *Otello* six years later, in his collaboration with Boito on another Shakespearean opera, where the jealous ravings of the Moor have become the comic rantings of Master Ford, and the motiveless malignity of Jago gives way to the very human frailties of that most benign of villains, Falstaff.

INDEX

Agamemnon, 71
American Imago, 120, 121
American Renaissance, 58
Among My Books, 97
Andrewes, Lancelot, 54n.
Antony and Cleopatra, 108, 112
Approaches to Shakespeare, 5n., 56
Archetypal Patterns in Poetry, 56
Aristotle, 5
Armed Vision, The, 3
Auden, W. H., 119

Bale, John, 9
Barber, C. L., 141, 142
Battenhouse, Roy, 56
Bible, The, 30, 37, 43, 48, 54n., 60, 160
"Billy Budd," 58
Boas, Guy, 55
Bodkin, Maud, 56, 137
Boito, Arrigo, 151–74 *passim*
Booth, Edwin, 23, 111, 112, 118, 167

Bradley, A. C., 5n., 8n., 25, 55, 75, 76, 131– 132, 146
Burke, Kenneth, 61, 68, 76, 117, 140

Campbell, Thomas, 94, 96
Chapman, George, 97
Character and Motive in Shakespeare, 121
Characteristics of Women, 93
Cinthio, Giovanbattista Giraldi, 101, 145, 167
Coleridge, Samuel Taylor, 3, 6, 56, 95, 104, 127– 129, 135, 136, 158
Contre-Machiavel, 122–3, 132, 163
Coventry Corpus Christi play, 11
Cowden-Clarke, Charles, 102
Cowden-Clarke, Mary, 102

Danby, John F., 132
Dante Alighieri, 32, 162

STANLEY EDGAR HYMAN

Stanley Edgar Hyman was a member of the literature faculty at Bennington College and a staff writer for *The New Yorker*. For some years in the 1960s he was lead reviewer for *The New Leader*. This book was written in England in 1969, on a sabbatical leave from Bennington College and a Guggenheim fellowship. He died suddenly at Bennington on 29 July 1970.